W9-ACJ-049

THIS WAITING FOR LOVE

Helene Johnson, 1931

All photos: Schlesinger Library, Radcliffe Institute, Harvard University

This Waiting for Love

HELENE JOHNSON

Poet of the Harlem Renaissance

Edited with an introduction by Verner D. Mitchell

Foreword by Cheryl A. Wall

Afterword by Abigail McGrath

University of Massachusetts Press Amherst

Printed in the United States of America
LC 00-055180
ISBN 1-55849-256-9
Designed by Kristina Kachele
Set in Monotype Joanna with Futura and Johann Sparkling display
by Keystone Typesetting, Inc.
Printed and bound by Sheridan Books, Inc.

Library of Congress Cataloging-in-Publication Data
Johnson, Helene, 1906–1995.
This waiting for love : Helene Johnson, poet of the Harlem Renaissance / edited and with an introduction by Verner D. Mitchell ; foreword by Cheryl A. Wall ; afterword by Abigail McGrath.
p. cm.
Includes all of the author's published poems and a selection of correspondence.
Includes bibliographical references.
ISBN 1-55849-256-9 (alk. paper)
1. Afro-American women—Poetry. 2. Johnson, Helene, 1906–1995—Correspondence. 3. Afro-American women poets—Correspondence. 4. Poets, American—20th century—Correspondence. 5. Afro-Americans—Poetry. 6. Love poetry, American. 7. Feminism—Poetry. 8. Harlem Renaissance. 9. New York (N.Y.)—Poetry. I. Mitchell, Verner D., 1957– II. Title.
PS3560.O37834 A6 2000
811'.54—dc21
[B] 00-055180
British Library Cataloguing in Publication data are available.

TO THE MEMORY OF HELENE JOHNSON

Contents

Foreword

"Chromatic Words": *The Poetry of Helene Johnson*

In many years of teaching courses on the Harlem Renaissance, I have learned to look forward to the days I introduce Helene Johnson's poems to my students. Few have heard of her, and almost none have encountered her work. But their delight in her poems almost never fails to equal my own. Two of Johnson's lyrics are among my favorites: "Sonnet to a Negro in Harlem" and "Poem."

Addressing the young migrant, newly arrived in Harlem, the sonneteer proclaims:

> You are disdainful and magnificent—
> Your perfect body and your pompous gait,
> Your dark eyes flashing solemnly with hate;
> Small wonder that you are incompetent
> To imitate those whom you so despise—

The qualities of contempt and resplendence reinforce each other, even as they repel and attract those passersby who hold the Negro in their gaze. If the poem's subject is destined never to adapt to urban life, he finds solace in the fierceness of his pride. My students applaud the swagger and recognize the rage. So does the speaker who concludes, "You are too splendid for this city street!" Despite its dated references to palm trees and "barbaric" song, the sonnet's representation of alienation in the inner city seems as current as hip-hop.

My other favorite is tied more tightly to its time. "Poem" celebrates the African American popular culture that so defined the zeitgeist of the 1920s that the decade was dubbed the Jazz Age. Written in free verse black vernacular, the poem addresses the crooning, tap-dancing, process-wearing, banjo-playing "jazz prince," who inspires it. But the poem's language collapses the distance between audience and performer. The terms of address are deeply personal: "Gee, boy, I love the way you hold your head / and the way you sing, and dance, / And everything." "Poem" is a performance piece, one in which Helene Johnson responds to the call of the musicians she has admired on the stage of Harlem's Lafayette Theater. As my students perform it in class, I think they begin to understand better the pride and exhilaration that defined the moment "when Harlem was in vogue."[1]

The ease with which Johnson moves from the rigor of the sonnet to the free idiom of "your shoulders jerking the jig-wa" is impressive. So too is the grace with which she slips the yoke of racial politics. Johnson offers no apologies for her love of laughter, dance, music, and color. While she seems always aware of a larger clash of cultures, she is impatient with constraints imposed on the behavior of ordinary people ostensibly for reasons of progress or propriety. She seems to recognize that these constraints in fact reflect racist and sexist thinking. Yet Johnson never seems to take herself or her "situation" too seriously. The leavening of humor is ever at hand. Consequently, it is always a disappointment to have to tell my students that Helene Johnson was a poet of great promise, who wrote only a handful of poems and who, like several other mysterious women, disappeared from the Harlem Renaissance leaving barely a trace.

This Waiting For Love comes then as an unexpected and most welcome gift. Here Verner Mitchell has collected all thirty-four of Helene Johnson's published poems, many of which have not been reprinted since they first appeared in various small magazines of the 1920s and 1930s: *The Saturday Evening Quill, Palms, Opportunity, Harlem,* and *Challenge*. Even many of us who are Johnson admirers do not know poems like "Night," "Cui Bono?," "Regalia," and "Futility," the poem that gives this volume its title. Moreover, those poems we recognize including "Bottled," "Fulfillment," "A Missionary Brings a Young Native to America," and "A Southern Road" seem new in the context of this volume. Not only does the imagery of "A Southern Road" anticipate the imagery of Billie Holiday's famous song "Strange Fruit," but its use of religious metaphors to protest lynching also looks back to poems by Claude McKay and forward to those by Gwendolyn Brooks. Johnson's statement is distinctive nonetheless. "Invocation" and "Summer Matures" explore the erotic, but from a safe distance. In the former, distance derives from the poem's many classical allusions; in the latter, the speaker invokes flora and fauna "riotous, rampant, wild and free," but only to cover her grave. As I reread "Magula," one of Johnson's most richly textured poems, the phrase "chromatic words" struck me as a perfect gloss for my two favorite poems. Color and music are what they evoke for me.

In addition to the poems and an excellent introduction that locates Helene Johnson's work in the context of the Harlem Renaissance, Verner Mitchell has compiled a chronology of her life that begins to lift the veil that she placed over it. She guarded her privacy so jealously that it was only in the 1970s that scholars discovered her married name, though she had wed William Warner Hubbell in 1933. I well remember my excitement in February 1987, when I read a brief notice in the

New York Times that announced a reading of the works by "one of the last surviving Harlem Renaissance poets." It had taken place the night before. At the time I was doing research for my book, *Women of the Harlem Renaissance*. Every reference I consulted gave only the same few facts about Johnson's girlhood, just as every anthology reprinted the same few poems. I had often wondered whether Johnson was still alive. Reading that notice I could scarcely believe that she had given a poetry reading—or—that I had missed it.[2] Immediately, I called the theater where the reading had taken place. The manager gave me the name and number of Johnson's daughter, Abigail McGrath, who told me that her eighty-year-old mother declined to be interviewed but suggested that I send any questions that I had in writing. Many months later, Johnson returned my questionnaire. The handwritten answers were too brief not to seem grudging. Everything about the exchange made me feel that my inquiries were invasive. Despite my disappointment, I could not help but admire Johnson's finely honed sense of irony. In response to my final question that asked if she were surprised by the continuing interest in the Harlem Renaissance, Johnson answered sharply: "never surprised by repetition."

I have good reason, therefore, to be impressed by the amount of new information that Verner Mitchell has uncovered about Johnson's life. Here are fresh facts concerning her childhood, one that she shared with her cousin, who grew up to be the novelist Dorothy West. These discoveries complicate the conventional wisdom about their privileged background. Here too is correspondence between Johnson, West, and Zora Neale Hurston, who sublet her New York apartment to the cousins while she collected folklore in the South. Hurston had met Johnson and West when all were feted at *Opportunity* magazine's Second Annual Literary Awards Dinner in May 1926. As Mitchell documents, their friendship outlasted the Harlem Renaissance. In addition to her links to Hurston and West,

Mitchell uncovers important connections between Johnson and other literary and visual artists, including Gwendolyn Bennett, Lois Mailou Jones, and Wallace Thurman.

Johnson's last published poem, "Let Me Sing My Song," appeared in 1935 in *Challenge*, the journal Dorothy West founded in an attempt to revive the spirit of the Harlem Renaissance. The journal was short-lived, despite a subsequent attempt by associate editor Richard Wright to ally it with radical politics. But Helene Johnson did not stop "singing." She ceased to publish but she continued to write. *This Waiting for Love* includes thirteen previously unpublished pieces. "He's About 22. I'm 63" (written circa 1970) offers irrefutable proof that Johnson's sense of humor remained intact.

After Helene Johnson died on 6 July 1995, the *New York Times* published an obituary that was accompanied by a selection of poems, under the heading "A Voice of Youth From a Renaissance." It was wonderful to see her legacy honored, even for one day. *This Waiting for Love* is an enduring tribute, one that provides the opportunity for a new generation of readers to discover the vibrant poetry of Helene Johnson. Answer the invitation that is extended to Magula:

> Oh Magula, come! Take my hand and I will read you
>   poetry,
> Chromatic words,
> Seraphic symphonies, . . .

CHERYL A. WALL
Rutgers University

1 Langston Hughes, *The Big Sea* (1940; reprint, New York: Hill and Wang, 1993), 227.

2 I have since learned that Johnson did not appear in person; instead, she recorded her poems on a tape, which she sent to the reading.

Acknowledgments

Working on this project has been an act of love, but I did not work alone. Thus I need to extend thanks to a number of persons, foremost the late Helene Johnson and Dorothy West. They courageously "defied the odds and put pen to paper when the century was young."

I am deeply grateful both to Helene Johnson's daughter, Abigail McGrath, for permitting me to publish her mother's work, and to my mentor, Cheryl A. Wall, for her long-standing support and guidance. I also thank the Schomburg Center for Research in Black Culture, the Boston Public Library, Howard University's Moorland-Spingarn Research Center, and Harvard University's Schlesinger Library on the History of Women, particularly its coordinator of photographs, Marie-Hélène Gold.

Special thanks to my many colleagues who read and commented on various parts of the manuscript: Dave Boxwell, Shara McCallum, Lee Barnhill, David Blake, Mark Noe, Will Harris, Mark Braley, and particularly Donald Anderson and Patrick Dooley. My gratitude to the two anonymous manuscript readers for their generous, detailed comments. And for their enduring patience and wise counsel, I thank, at the University of Massachusetts Press, Stephanie Attia, Clark Dougan, and Bruce Wilcox.

Finally, for their boundless love, inspiration, and support, I thank my friends and family, most especially my wife and best friend, Veronica Robbin, and our children, Jared and Courtney.

V. D. M.

Introduction

Students of the Harlem Renaissance have long appreciated Helene Johnson's talent. But because so many of her poems are located in older, often inaccessible journals (*Challenge, Fire!!, Harlem, The Messenger, Palms,* and so on) teaching and even reading her work has been difficult. Eugene B. Redmond accordingly captures a long-standing sentiment in his 1976 study, *Drumvoices: The Mission of Afro-American Poetry.* He dubs Johnson an important minor poet whose entire "output should be collected and published in book form."[1] The following volume, *This Waiting for Love,* is the first book ever published on Johnson and an answer to Redmond's call. The volume makes Johnson's poetry from the twenties and thirties, as well as previously unpublished poems from the sixties, seventies, and eighties, available to her many enthusiasts. More important, it brings Johnson's art to new generations of readers.

As the title *This Waiting for Love* suggests, Johnson's poems defy the genteel conventions that governed many early twentieth-century female writers. Her verse also offers a penetrating insight into 1920s America, particularly into the artistic community. Several of her poems respond to aesthetic and political conflicts during the Harlem Renaissance. They counter, for example (as does Langston Hughes's celebrated 1926 essay "The Negro Artist and the Racial Mountain"), the aesthetics of older writers such as Alain Locke and W.E.B. Du Bois. Recall Locke's comments about jazz: "Unfortunately, but temporarily, what is best known are the vulgarizations; and of these 'Jazz' and by-products are in the ascendancy."[2] Recall, too, Du Bois's caustic reaction to Claude McKay's 1928 novel *Home to Harlem:* "for the most part [it] nauseates me, and after the dirtier parts of its filth I feel distinctly like taking a bath."[3] Johnson's dialogue and dispute with members of the literary establishment make her, at a minimum, an important and powerful foremother. Her role can perhaps be best illustrated through a sustained reading of her 1926 poem "Magula." But first, some background information on the poet and on what some term the "radical" nature of her verse.

Johnson was born 7 July 1906, in Boston, Massachusetts, to Ella Benson Johnson, of Camden, South Carolina, and George William Johnson, of Nashville, Tennessee. She was an only child.[4] Shortly after her birth her parents separated, and thus she never knew her father or her father's parents. Her mother's parents, Benjamin Benson and Helen Pease Benson—after whom Johnson was named—had been born into slavery in South Carolina.[5]

> Mama [Johnson's grandmother] was born a slave, bound to obedience. . . . All too soon she was bound again. For at fifteen she was bound in marriage to my nineteen-year-old grandfather. . . . Then Mama was bound forever by her batches of babies, her girlhood over before it was ever experienced.[6]

After his wife's death, Benjamin Benson, a minister, followed three of his daughters—Ella, Minnie, and Rachel—north to Massachusetts. There he summered in the town of Oak Bluffs on Martha's Vineyard Island, and earned his living as a carpenter. Rachel's daughter and Johnson's first cousin, the novelist and short story writer Dorothy West, would later live in Oak Bluffs (on property bought by her grandfather Benjamin Benson)[7] until her death in August 1998, at age ninety-one.

Johnson and West grew up together at 478 Brookline Avenue, in the Brookline section of Boston. They spent most of their summers at Oak Bluffs. As West explains, "The house that I grew up in was four-storied, but we were an extended family."[8]

My mother's mother had eighteen children, and, later on—because my father [a greengrocer in downtown Boston] was doing quite well—many of my mother's sisters and nephews and nieces came to live with us. All of us had different complexions—at one end there was a blond kid and at the other end there was me. . . . My mother was a light woman, and my Aunt Minnie looked white. Those were the two people who brought me up. There were four of us children. They were my first cousins. A blond kid, an olive-skinned kid, a golden-skin kid, and me.[9]

Johnson, the eldest of the cousins, was the golden-skin kid. She was also the prototype for the character Vicky, in West's novel *The Living Is Easy.* Chapter 19 of the novel captures the excited little cousins on a Christmas morning: "Victoria was the first to scamper out of bed, where she lay beside Lily, her mother. Vicky was seven, a tall, butter-colored, red-cheeked child, whose seniority of six months over Penny [Aunt Minnie's daughter, Jean] and ten months over Judy [Dorothy West] made her the unquestioned leader of the little girls."[10] Chapter 29 presents the cousins, now fifth-graders, as avid readers and aspiring writers: "Restless, fun loving Vicky could be sobered and inspired by the simple act of opening a book. She turned pages tenderly, not wanting to break the ebony thread that wove itself into a wonderful pattern of words. And the words were the explanation of life, the key to understanding. She, the child of Cleo's [Aunt Rachel's] heart, was the child whose intelligence equaled Cleo's hope."[11]

According to T. J. Bryan, Johnson "credited her early interest in writing to her mother, who provided her with new experiences; to the supplemental education she received at home; and to her exploration of library books."[12] Johnson and West attended Boston's Lafayette School, the Martin School, and the prestigious Boston Girls' Latin School. After Girls' Latin, they took writing courses at Boston University and joined The Saturday Evening Quill Club, an organization of aspiring black Boston writers. The 1929 number of the club's annual, *The Saturday Evening Quill*, features West's story "Prologue to a Life" as well as seven of Johnson's poems.

In April of 1926, the cousins, now ages nineteen and eighteen, traveled from Boston to New York City for a brief visit. The following year, still full of zest and awe, they returned to the city. This time the cousins came to stay and to continue their education, enrolling in Columbia University's Extension Division, where they studied with the novelist John Erskine.[13] Soon after their move, they were ushered gently into the heart of Harlem's literary renaissance by the able and witty raconteur Zora Neale Hurston. Wallace Thurman's satirical roman à clef, *Infants of the Spring* (1932), presents Hurston as Sweetie May Carr and famously details the cousins' entrance:

> Sweetie May was accompanied by two young girls, recently emigrated from Boston. They were the latest to be hailed incipient immortals. Their names were Doris Westmore [West] and Hazel Jamison [Johnson]. Doris wrote short stories. Hazel wrote poetry. . . . Raymond [Thurman] liked them more than he did most of the younger recruits to the movement. For one thing, they were characterized by a freshness and naïveté which he and his cronies had lost. And, surprisingly enough for Negro prodigies, they actually gave promise of possessing literary talent.[14]

The events that led them to move, in West's words, to "the magical city of New York" had been set in motion three years earlier.[15] Toward the end of 1924 Johnson submitted a poem, "Trees at Night," to the Urban League's official magazine, *Opportunity*. Her poem was accepted for publication and eventually appeared in the journal. Then, when the Urban League held its first annual literary awards ceremony in May 1925, "Trees at

Night" won an honorable mention. Encouraged by her success, Johnson decided to enter three poems in the 1926 contest, and West, at Johnson's urging, penned and submitted a short story. West reports that in due time they received invitations to the awards ceremony, and they were "overwhelmed with joy."[16]

They persuaded their parents—Rachel and Isaac West and Ella Johnson—to let them go to New York City to attend the awards dinner on May 1. Neither was disappointed. Johnson's "Fulfillment," "Magula," and "The Road," won first, fourth, and seventh honorable mentions, and West's "The Typewriter" shared the second-place prize for fiction along with Hurston's short story "Muttsy." For West, sharing the prize with the older writer was unsettling, but, as she explains, that initial, somewhat awkward meeting resulted in a lifelong friendship:

> God, with whom I had lengthy conversations in my childhood and presumed had got to know me and my aspirations, allowed me to share a second prize with the now legendary Zora Neale Hurston. At first she had mixed feelings about sharing a prize with an unknown teenager. But in time I became her little sister, and my affection for her has never diminished. In time I was to play my part in the Harlem Renaissance. I was nineteen and its youngest member.[17]

Thus at the 1926 *Opportunity* awards dinner, cousins West and Johnson began their long friendship with Zora Neale Hurston. And in so doing, they received their first taste of Harlem's magic.[18]

West has been best known for her 1948 novel *The Living Is Easy*, although she is currently in the midst of a literary rebirth, owing to her well-received memoir *The Richer, The Poorer: Stories, Sketches, and Reminiscences* (1995), and her best-selling 1995 novel *The Wedding*. She finished the latter work with the help of her Martha's Vineyard neighbor Jacqueline Onassis. "To the memory of my editor, Jacqueline Kennedy Onassis," reads the book's gracious dedication. "Though there was never such a mismatched pair in appearance, we were perfect partners." "It's interesting that so much is happening and so many people have called," West beamed in a 1995 interview. "At my age it didn't have to happen."[19]

Johnson, by contrast, is still relatively unknown. Surely much of her popular and critical neglect can be explained by the fact that heretofore there has been no available volume of her writings. Also, unlike West, who continued to write (and never married), Johnson took a lengthy hiatus from her writing when she married William Hubbell and had to help support her family. The couple's only child, Abigail McGrath, recalls her father working for the Brooklyn shipyard and her mother working both inside the home and outside, as a civil service employee. Years later, speaking of the writer's need for "a certain laxity," Johnson explained: "It's very difficult for a poor person to be that unfastened. They have to eat. In order to eat, you have to be fastened and tightly. . . . [Y]ou don't have too much time to go in another direction. And to write anything (it can be poetry or anything at all), you have to have time. You have to sit and rock like a fool or look out the window, and something will come by."[20] Johnson last published a poem in May 1935, two years after her marriage.

Over the years, Johnson generally remained out of the public eye. Always painfully shy, she declined an invitation to give a public poetry reading (at New York City's Off Center Theater) as recently as February 1987, at age eighty.[21] The following year, West's wide-ranging interview with Katrine Dalsgård shed light on the cousins' early days in Manhattan. We learned, for example, that after arriving in the city, they shared a room at the Harlem YWCA. Later, when "Zora got a grant [and] went South," recalls West, "Helene and I took over her apartment."[22] West also discussed their friendships with such luminaries as Claude McKay, A'Lelia Walker, Wallace Thurman, Carl Van Vechten, Countee Cullen, and Langston Hughes.

From the early 1960s to the early 1980s, Johnson lived at 210 Thompson Street, her "dream" apartment in Greenwich Village. She always loved Greenwich Village, and she particularly enjoyed the young people she came to know from her outings to Judson Poet's Theater and Washington Square Park (both two blocks from her apartment).[23] With the exception of a few years on Cape Cod in the 1980s, Johnson lived her entire adult life (over half a century) in New York City. She died in Manhattan on July 6, 1995, the day before her eighty-ninth birthday.[24]

Four years younger than poets Gwendolyn Bennett and Langston Hughes, Johnson is described in the July 1926 edition of *Opportunity* as "perhaps the youngest of the new group of Negro poets" (232). Miss Johnson "possesses true lyric talent," observed James Weldon Johnson in 1931. "She is one of the younger group who has taken . . . the 'racial' bull by the horns. She has taken the very qualities and circumstances that have long called for apology or defense and extolled them in an unaffected manner."[25] Over a half century later, Patricia Liggins Hill notes that "Johnson's racial poems established her during the 1920s as one of the brightest lights shining among the up-and-coming young poets. One has to wonder," she adds, "what the literary fate of this talented poet would have been if she had received the patronage and critical attention enjoyed by several of the male poets of the time."[26] Similarly, in a 1998 interview, the Pulitzer Prize–winning poet Yusef Komunyakaa observes that Johnson was the youngest and most talented of the Harlem Renaissance poets. "It's a shame," he continues, "that she was unable to reconcile the demands of working nine to five and writing."[27]

Another who sang Johnson's praise was a judge for the 1926 *Opportunity* contest, Robert Frost. Frost called Johnson's "The Road" the "finest" poem submitted.[28] Perhaps he thought that Johnson's "nature" poems, set in her beloved New England, echoed his! "The Road," also reminiscent of Whitman's "Song of the Open Road," uses nature as a controlling metaphor in a captivating expression of racial pride. Most of Johnson's early poems (published between May 1925 and June 1926) focus on nature. Trees become "Slim Sentinels / Stretching lacy arms / About a slumbrous moon" in "Trees at Night"; the sea in "Metamorphism" is "This sudden birth of unrestrained splendor." And in "Fulfillment," a poet longs

> To climb a hill that hungers for the sky,
> To dig my hands wrist deep in pregnant earth,
> To watch a young bird, veering, learn to fly,
> To give a still, stark poem shining birth.

After Johnson moved to New York City, she saw poverty up close—witnessing, in particular, the hard time African Americans had, and personally experiencing the glass ceiling. In time, she drifted away from the lighthearted nature verse, and, notes her daughter, "her personality became more radical, politically, socially, and economically."

When contemplating how to organize the poems in this collection, I considered arranging them chronologically within three thematic categories: Nature, Race and Gender, and Love. The difficulty, of course, is that thematic groupings always overlap. In which group, for instance, would one place "A Southern Road," a poem that protests a lynching, but a poem whose controlling metaphor is a beautiful southern road? Because so many of Johnson's poems resist thematic categories, I eventually decided simply to present them according to their original publication dates. An advantage to this chronological arrangement is that the reader will be able to study the progression and evolution of Johnson's poetics.

I take the book's title from the brief 1926 poem "Futility."

It is silly—
This waiting for love
In a parlor.
When love is singing up and down the alley
Without a collar.

Like Andrew Marvell's "To His Coy Mistress" and Gwendolyn Brooks's "a song in the front yard," "Futility" renders a ringing endorsement of love without coyness or shame. And in rejecting bourgeois rituals of courtship, it exemplifies the air of defiant sensuality present in so much of Johnson's verse.

Although her love poetry usually focuses on erotic themes, Johnson also deals with less controversial images of love. Her octave "Mother," to cite one example, meditates on a mother's love of Christ and the intense love shared by mother and daughter. At the opposite end of the spectrum, and thematically more representative of Johnson's verse, are "The Little Love," "Cui Bono?," "Foraging," "He's about 22. I'm 63," and the long dramatic monologue "Widow with a Moral Obligation." In the latter work, the widow, having sensed the presence of her long dead husband, runs away from her new "friend." I quote the opening lines:

Won't you come again, my friend?
I'll not be so shy.
I shall have a candle lit
To light you by.
I shall have my hair unbound,
My gown undone,
And we shall have a night of love
And death in one.

I was very foolish
To have run away before,
But you see I thought I heard
Him knocking at the door . . .

As the above poems partially illustrate, Johnson's preferred form was the free verse of Whitman or Hughes, rather than the more formal structures of the nineteenth-century British Romantics, preferred by Cullen and to a lesser extent by McKay. Nonetheless, on occasion, she did write sonnets. Her favorite subjects were love, protest, female sexual awakenings, the importance of the African past, the sensuousness of nature, and black cultural pride—matters considered inappropriate by the genteel readers of the early twentieth century. Indeed, Johnson's willingness to challenge accepted boundaries—both aesthetic and political—is likely the most prominent feature of her poetry.

I conclude my introduction with a reading of one of Johnson's more overtly political poems, "Magula." This poem succinctly illustrates the "radical" nature of Johnson's verse. As critic Maureen Honey notes, "The radical nature of [Johnson's] poetry lies not only in its employ of what was considered nonpoetic language, but also in Johnson's praise of those aspects of Black culture most despised by whites. She loved insouciance, sensuality, vivacity, and celebrated them."[29]

"Magula" was first published in the October 1926 number of *Palms*. The list of contributors to this special issue, guest edited by Countee Cullen, reads like a Harlem Renaissance "Who's Who." Established writers Jessie Fauset, Du Bois, Locke, William Stanley Braithwaite, Georgia Douglas Johnson, and Anne Spencer contributed pieces, as did several of the younger ones: Gwendolyn Bennett, Walter White, Arna Bontemps, Bruce Nugent, Clarissa Scott Delaney, Langston Hughes, and, of course, Helene Johnson.

Subsequent collections in which "Magula" appeared, from *Caroling Dusk: An Anthology of Verse by Negro Poets* in 1927, to *Shadowed Dreams: Women's Poetry of the Harlem Renaissance* in 1989, incorrectly identify the poem as "Magalu." I have retained Johnson's original spelling. The poem is a free-verse dramatization of the inner mythic "good person / bad person" struggle for the titular character's heart and soul. To that end, it dramatizes a metaphoric tug-of-love for an African woman's affections. Johnson adeptly delays the moment of confrontation, creating first an expectation of pleasure with the two-word sentence, "Summer comes." Against this background, the poem sprinkles animated images of the natural world. At this level it caters to shallow consumers of Renaissance literary production, giving them exactly what they look for and want—a flashy, exotic vision of Africa. By poem's end, however, Johnson has deftly destabilized those expectations.

Summer comes.
The ziczac hovers
'Round the greedy-mouthed crocodile.
A vulture bears away a foolish jackal.
The flamingo is a dash of pink
Against dark green mangroves,
Her slender legs rivalling her slim neck.

The rich word play on "bears" invites interpretation. First, "bears" meshes harmoniously with the other animal appellations (ziczac, crocodile, vulture, jackal, flamingo); second, it shows the vulture "bearing" away the foolish jackal; and, third, it hints that the vulture and jackal are entwined in an intimate and fatal embrace ("bear" hug). Is the ziczac moments away from a similar fate? In drawing our attention to the flamingo's fragility and vulnerability—her slender legs and slim neck—the poem seems to support this reading. Such a reading suggests an extended analogy between the devoured or soon-to-be devoured animals and vulnerable Magula.

Critic Erlene Stetson posits a more upbeat reading. According to her, the ziczac is "an Egyptian species of plover who warns the crocodile of approaching danger by its cry."[30] Thus, the ziczac and crocodile are symbolic soul mates, and the ziczac's warning both foreshadows and parallels the speaker's plea to Magula. An added benefit of Stetson's reading is that it locates the poem in Africa. Consequently, the pretty flamingo, "a dash of pink / Against dark green mangroves," becomes a rich foil against the dark Magula:

> The laughing lake gurgles delicious music in its throat
> And lulls to sleep the lazy lizard,
> A nebulous being on a sun-scorched rock.
> In such a place,
> In this pulsing, riotous gasp of color,
> I met Magula, dark as a tree at night,
> Eager lipped, listening to a man with a white collar
> And a small black book with a cross on it.

In this world view, "dark" retains its pre-Western meaning; not a vehicle of fear and the demonic, darkness is a coequal member of the rainbow's "pulsing, riotous gasp of color." Danger then comes not from the darkness, but from the glaring absence of camouflage between pink/dark green, and dark/white. Threatening dark Magula is the "man with a white collar." His "small black book" is an enticing trap to dark Magula, but it is also an extension of the constraining collar which seeks to stifle Magula's dance.

The opening lines, then, are action-packed portraits of the African wild. There is an aura of danger, but this danger contributes a sense of excitement which is preferable to a staid and colorless (black book and white collar) world without dance.

Having established a static frame with the end-stopped "Summer comes," the poem rushes forward—hovering, bearing, rivalling, laughing, pulsing—toward the central meeting, when it again stops. All eyes, accordingly, converge on unprotected Magula.

Suggestive of 1920s Harlem, the laughing lake's soothing syncopation vibrates with "delicious music," lulling the lazy lizard to sleep. Magula, too, is susceptible to hypnosis. But unlike the laughing lake's emancipating rhythms, the music produced by the man is foreign, unnatural, and confining. Therefore the poem forcefully rejects the constraining, universalizing polemic of the white collar and the black book. Notice that the "nebulous being on a sun-scorched rock," the chameleon-like lizard, unites with the speaker's chromatic words to embody the rainbow's "pulsing, riotous gasp of color." In contrast, the man with the white collar spurns diversity, seeing only in black and white, and offering a creed that will not let Magula dance. Given the centrality of dance to African culture, any creed which rejects dance would be psychically and physically harmful for Magula. Critic Beverley Bryan, writing in *The Heart of the Race* (1986), correctly discerns the importance of dance in African culture: "Alongside music, dance has been our most important form of cultural expression. . . . Historically dance has always been integral to Black culture. There is literally a dance for everything, back in the land of our ancestors—a dance for death, for birth, for weddings, for social occasions, for everything you can imagine."[31]

Next, the poem's "I" enters, offering—with Whitmanesque affection—poetry that can rescue Magula from the alien tempter with the white collar:

> Oh Magula, come! Take my hand and I will read you
>   poetry,
> Chromatic words,

Seraphic symphonies,
Fill your throat with laughter and your heart with song.
Do not let him lure you from your laughing waters,
Lulling lakes, lissome winds.
Would you sell the colors of your sunset and fragrance
Of your flowers, and the passionate wonder of your forest
For a creed that will not let you dance?

Clearly the speaker is a poetic guide who can lead Magula away from that which threatens her. But precisely where will the speaker steer Magula? Exploring possible answers to this question will show the boldness and beauty of Johnson's artistic vision.

During the antebellum era, black women were stereotyped as loyal mammies who were innately equipped only for nursing white children, scrubbing floors, and an array of other domestic chores that their "delicate" mistresses would not perform. In point of fact, from John Wheatley's Massachusetts to Thomas Jefferson's Monticello, "faithful" black females were forced to tend other people's households. By the time of Johnson's writings, however, the stereotype had curiously become inverted. No longer dependable mammies, black women were now seen as lascivious and sexually insatiable, unsafe near any household.[32] Thus, when the poetic guide implores Magula to realize the beauty of her flowers and the passionate wonder of her forest, the guide is rejecting societally imposed definitions and constraints for black female sexuality and personhood. Defiantly shunning the man's creed, the wise guide seeks to focus Magula's attention to the wonder of her laughing waters, lulling lakes, lissome winds: natural bridges leading to the deepest sites of passion and wholeness. Once secure in the loving embrace of her own forest, Magula's heart will blossom with song and her feet with dance.

Some, no doubt fearful that artistic explorations of passion would fuel negative stereotypes, strove to mute the black music and dance. The distinguished Harlem Renaissance philosopher and Rhodes Scholar Alain Locke, for example, described jazz as "a submerged and half-inarticulate motive in Negro doggerel," a "mere trickery of syncopation." Similarly, he called the "Jazz school" of Negro poetry a "vulgarization."[33] Writing in his "New Negro" essay of 1925, Locke insists that socially conscious artists should eschew vulgar forms so they can then function as "the advance-guard of the African peoples" to rehabilitate "the race in world esteem. . . . The especially cultural recognition they win should in turn prove the key to that revaluation of the Negro which must precede or accompany any considerable further betterment of race relationships."[34] "Magula's" appearance in October of 1926 clearly indicates that Johnson was unwilling to suppress the colors of her sunset or to adhere to any creed that would not let her dance.

Later that same year (1926) Johnson and Hurston helped organize the avant-garde journal *Fire!!*, subtitled *A Quarterly Devoted to the Younger Negro Artists*. Its inaugural issue featured a number of erotic drawings, Wallace Thurman's vignette of a sixteen-year-old prostitute "Cordelia the Crude," Gwendolyn Bennett's "Wedding Day," the story of a former boxer and jazz musician left at the altar by a white prostitute, and Richard Bruce Nugent's "Smoke, Lilies, and Jade," the first African American work to openly explore homosexuality.[35] By challenging forthrightly the Victorian sensibilities of Locke and others in the black literary establishment, the publication of *Fire!!* was the culminating act of a movement that Arnold Rampersad describes (in something of an overstatement) as the students, the younger writers, dispensing with their dean, Alain Locke.[36]

In noting that Helene Johnson's "imagination was clearly activated by the sights and sounds of jazz age Harlem," Maureen Honey endorses my interpretation of a Magula at home, both in the vibrant and exciting world of Harlem's Jazz Age, and beside the "laughing waters, / Lulling lakes, lissome winds" of dark Africa. Concerning "Magula," she writes that "the speaker warns a young African woman not to be seduced by a missionary to whom she is eagerly listening."[37] Although Honey's reading is convincing, Johnson's rich art resists restrictive interpretations, demanding that it be viewed from several different angles, open to many perspectives. How, for example, do we know that Magula is a woman? The flamingo is female, and the man is definitely male, but the poem provides no other references to gender. The poem goes to considerable lengths to sidestep gender; in fact, the "I" narrator is arguably both and neither male/female, much like the narrator of Toni Morrison's *Jazz*. Furthermore, the name Magula is indeterminate, one which resists gender constructions. From this perspective, Magula becomes a composite of dark youth—both male and female. And poet Johnson is seeking to save not just one child, but an entire race, an entire people. It is here in Johnson's goal that I find the compelling vitality of her art.

This Waiting for Love recognizes Helene Johnson as an important literary foremother. It celebrates the import of her life and art. Now her laughing lake can gurgle its delicious music to all Magulas present and future.

Notes to Introduction

1 Eugene B. Redmond, *Drumvoices: The Mission of Afro-American Poetry, A Critical History* (Garden City, N.Y.: Anchor, 1976), 207.

2 Alain Locke, "The Negro in American Culture" (1929), in *Black Voices*, ed. Abraham Chapman (New York: Mentor, 1968), 524.

3 W.E.B. Du Bois, "Two Novels," *The Crisis* 35 (June 1928): 202.

4 Cheryl A. Wall, unpublished mail interview with Helene Johnson, June 1987.

5 T. J. Bryan, "Helene Johnson," in *Notable Black American Women*, ed. Jessie Carney Smith (Detroit: Gale, 1992), 587.

6 Dorothy West, *The Richer, the Poorer: Stories, Sketches, and Reminiscences* (New York: Anchor, 1995), 186.

7 Bryan, "Helene Johnson," 587.

8 West, *The Richer, The Poorer,* 167.

9 Rachel West lists her mother's and stepmother's nineteen children, some of whom died in infancy, from oldest to youngest: Robert, Wilkie, David, Ella, Carrie (also known as Dolly), Rachel, Mattie, Isabella, Minnie, Bennie, Jessie, Scotter, Eugene, Scipio, Emma, Belton, Sarah, Malcom, and Ruth (Dorothy West Papers, Schlesinger Library, Harvard University). Quoted in Katrine Dalsgård, "Alive and Well and Living on the Island of Martha's Vineyard: An Interview with Dorothy West, October 29, 1988," *The Langston Hughes Review* 12.2 (Fall 1993): 29, 32.

10 West, *The Living Is Easy* (1948; reprint, New York: The Feminist Press, 1982), 198.

11 Ibid., 299–300.

12 Bryan, "Helene Johnson," 589.

13 Gwendolyn Bennett, "The Ebony Flute," *Opportunity* (December 1926): 391; (January 1927); 28–29.

14 Thurman, *Infants of the Spring* (1932; reprint, Boston: Northeastern University Press, 1992), 230–31.

15 West, *The Richer, the Poorer,* 2.

16 Ibid., 2.

17 Ibid., 2–3.

18 On May 7, 1927, during *Opportunity's* third and final literary contest, West received a Buckner Award for her story "An Unimportant Man." Johnson's "Summer Matures" and "Sonnet to a Negro in Harlem" won the second and fourth prizes for poetry, respectively. For a list of award winners for all three years, see *Opportunity* (May 1925): 142–43; (May 1926): 156–57; (June 1927): 179.

19 Quoted in V. R. Peterson, "Talking with . . . Dorothy West," *People* 43 (March 6, 1995): 36–37. In August 1997, another first lady, Mrs. Hillary Clinton, traveled to Oak Bluffs and helped West celebrate her ninetieth birthday. The event was televised internationally on Cable News Network.

20 Quoted in Bryan, "Helene Johnson," 590. Abigail McGrath discussed her mother's life and art with me during telephone interviews conducted in January 2000.

21 "Poetry," *New York Times* (February 8, 1987): C13. The event was scheduled to help launch the City's Black History Month festivities. Abigail McGrath founded the Off Center Theater with her husband, Tony McGrath.

22 Dalsgård, *Alive and Well,* 30.

23 Abigail McGrath, during a telephone interview with author, January 2000. In the 1960s, Judson Poet's Theater (now Judson Memorial Church) was a hub of experimental theater, music, and dance.

24 Abigail McGrath and "Obituary," *New York Times* (11 July 1995).

25 J. W. Johnson, *The Book of American Negro Poetry* (1931; reprint, New York: Harcourt, 1983), 279.

26 Patricia Liggins Hill, ed., *Call & Response: The Riverside Anthology of the African American Literary Tradition* (New York: Houghton Mifflin, 1998), 918.

27 In February 1998, Komunyakaa and I discussed Johnson at length.

28 Quoted in Gwendolyn Bennett, "The Ebony Flute," *Opportunity* (September 1926): 292.

29 Honey, "Introduction," *Shadowed Dreams: Women's Poetry of the Harlem Renaissance* (New Brunswick: Rutgers University Press, 1989), 28.

30 Erlene Stetson, *Black Sister: Poetry by Black American Women,* 1746–1980 (Bloomington: Indiana University Press, 1985), 79.

31 Beverley Bryan, Stella Dadzie, and Suzanne Scafe, eds. *The Heart of the Race: Black Women's Lives in Britain* (London: Virago Press, 1985), 202–3.

32 A more sustained examination of these two binary images, such as the one Patricia Hill Collins provides in *Black Feminist Thought: Knowledge, Consciousness, and the Politics of Empowerment* (New York: Routledge, 1991), shows that both stereotypes were actually produced and engendered, quite paradoxically, during American slavery.

33 Locke, "The Negro in American Culture," 524, 532.

34 Locke, "The New Negro," in *The New Negro: Voices of the Harlem Renaissance* (1925; reprint, New York: Macmillan, 1992), 5, 14–15.

35 This first and only issue of *Fire!!* also contains Hurston's play "Color Struck" and short story "Sweat" and Johnson's poem "A Southern Road."

36 Arnold Rampersad, *The Life of Langston Hughes* (New York: Oxford University Press, 1986), 135. For more on Locke and the Harlem Renaissance, see my essay "Alain Locke: Philosophical 'Mid-Wife' of the Harlem Renaissance," in *The Critical Pragmatism of Alain Locke*, ed. Leonard Harris (New York: Rowman & Littlefield, 1999), 191–98.

37 Honey, "Introduction," 28.

Poems

Trees at Night

Slim Sentinels
Stretching lacy arms
About a slumbrous moon;
Black quivering
Silhouettes,
Tremulous,
Stencilled on the petal
Of a bluebell;
Ink spluttered
On a robin's breast;
The jagged rent
Of mountains
Reflected in a
Stilly sleeping lake;
Fragile pinnacles
Of fairy castles;
Torn webs of shadows;
And
Printed 'gainst the sky—
The trembling beauty
Of an urgent pine.

Opportunity (May 1925): 147. Awarded Honorable Mention.

My Race

Ah my race,
Hungry race,
Throbbing and young—
Ah, my race,
Wonder race,
Sobbing with song—
Ah, my race,
Laughing race,
Careless in mirth—
Ah, my veiled race
Unformed race,
Fumbling in birth.

Opportunity (July 1925): 196.

The Road

Ah, little road all whirry in the breeze,
A leaping clay hill lost among the trees,
The bleeding note of rapture steaming thrush
Caught in a drowsy hush
And stretched out in a single singing line of dusky song.

Ah little road, brown as my race is brown,
Your trodden beauty like our trodden pride,
Dust of the dust, they must not bruise you down.
Rise to one brimming golden, spilling cry!

The New Negro (1925): 300.
Opportunity (July 1926): 225. Awarded Honorable Mention.
Caroling Dusk (1927): 221.
The Book of American Negro Poetry (1931): 280.

Night

The moon flung down the bower of her hair,
A sacred cloister while she knelt at prayer.
She crossed pale bosom, breathed a sad amen—
Then bound her hair about her head again.

Opportunity (January 1926): 26.

Metamorphism

Is this the sea?
This calm emotionless bosom,
Serene as the heart of a converted Magdalene—
Or this?
This lisping, lulling murmur of soft waters
Kissing a white beached shore with tremulous lips;
Blue rivulets of sky gurgling deliciously
O'er pale smooth stones—
This too?
This sudden birth of unrestrained splendor,
Tugging with turbulent force at Neptune's leash;
This passionate abandon,
This strange tempestuous soliloquy of Nature,
All these—the sea?

Opportunity (March 1926): 81.

Fulfillment

To climb a hill that hungers for the sky,
   To dig my hands wrist deep in pregnant earth,
To watch a young bird, veering, learn to fly,
   To give a still, stark poem shining birth.

To hear the rain drool, dimpling, down the drain
   And splash with a wet giggle in the street,
To ramble in the twilight after supper,
   And to count the pretty faces that you meet.

To ride to town on trolleys, crowded, teaming
   With joy and hurry and laughter and push and sweat—
Squeezed next to a patent-leathered Negro dreaming
   Of a wrinkled river and a minnow net.

To buy a paper from a breathless boy,
   And read of kings and queens in foreign lands,
Hyperbole of romance and adventure,
   All for a penny the color of my hand.

To lean against a strong tree's bosom, sentient
   And hushed before the silent prayer it breathes,
To melt the still snow with my seething body
   And kiss the warm earth tremulous underneath.

Ah, life, to let your stabbing beauty pierce me
   And wound me like we did the studded Christ,
To grapple with you, loving you too fiercely,
   And to die bleeding—consummate with Life.

Opportunity (June 1926): 194. Awarded First Honorable Mention.

Fiat Lux*

Her eyes had caught a bit of loveliness—
A flower blooming in the prison yard.
She ran to it and pressed it to her lips,
This Godsend of a land beyond the walls;
She drank its divine beauty with her kiss—

A guard wrested the flower from her hand,
With awful art, her humble back laid bare—
Soft skin, and darker than a dreamless night;
He tossed aside the burden of her hair.
"I'll teach you to pick flowers in this yard.
They ain't for niggers." He began to flog.

Her pale palmed hands grasped the thin air in quest.
Until, like two antalgic† words, they fell,
And whispered something to her bleeding breast.
And she forgot the misery of her back.
Somehow she knew that God, HER God was there—
That what was pain was but her striped flesh.
Her soul, inviolate, was havened in prayer.
On a cross of bigotry she was crucified
Because she was not white. And like her Father
On the holyrood,‡ whispered, "Forgive."
And in her eyes there shone a Candlemas light.
He flung the whip into the flower bed,
He did not even note that she was dead.

The Messenger (July 1926): 199.
Opportunity (December 1928): 361 [revision].

*Latin for "let there be light."
†Tending to prevent or alleviate pain.
‡A crucifix; the cross on which Jesus died.

The Little Love

A shy ear bared
For incipient kisses;
A secret shared
In laughter exquisite;
Soft finger tips,
While the night embraces,
Touch passionate colors
That morning erases.
And when the Dawn wakens,
No attempt to recapture
Those swift fleeting hours of ecstatic rapture,
But hide the shy ear with a curl, my pet,
And that little secret,—forget.

The Messenger (July 1926): 203.

Futility

It is silly—
This waiting for love
In a parlor.
When love is singing up and down the alley
Without a collar.

Opportunity (August 1926): 259.

Mother

Soft hair faintly white where the angels touch it;
Pale candles flaming in her eyes
Hallowing her vision of Christ;
And yet I know
She would break each Commandment
Against her heart,
And bury them pointed and jagged in her soul—
That I may smile.

Opportunity (September 1926): 295.

Love in Midsummer

Ah love
Is like a throbbing wind,
A lullaby all crooning,
Ah love
Is like a summer sea's soft breast.
Ah love's
A sobbing violin
That naïve night is tuning,
Ah love
Is down from off the white moon's nest.

The Messenger (October 1926): 311.

Magula

Summer comes.
The ziczac hovers
Round the greedy-mouthed crocodile.
A vulture bears away a foolish jackal.
The flamingo is a dash of pink
Against dark green mangroves,
Her slender legs rivalling her slim neck.
The laughing lake gurgles delicious music in its throat
And lulls to sleep the lazy lizard,
A nebulous being on a sun-scorched rock.
In such a place,
In this pulsing, riotous gasp of color,
I met Magula, dark as a tree at night,
Eager-lipped, listening to a man with a white collar
And a small black book with a cross on it.
Oh Magula, come! Take my hand and I'll read you poetry,
Chromatic words,
Seraphic symphonies,
Fill up your throat with laughter and your heart with
song.
Do not let him lure you from your laughing waters,
Lulling lakes, lissom winds.
Would you sell the colors of your sunset and the fragrance
Of your flowers, and the passionate wonder of your forest
For a creed that will not let you dance?

Palms (October 1926): 23.
Caroling Dusk (1927): 223–24.

A Southern Road

Yolk-colored tongue
parched beneath a burning sky,
A lazy little tune
Hummed up the crest of some
Soft sloping hill.
One streaming line of beauty
Flowing by a forest
Pregnant with tears.
A hidden nest for beauty
Idly flung by God
In one lonely lingering hour
Before the Sabbath.
A blue-fruited black gum,
Like a tall predella,*
Bears a dangling figure,—
Sacrificial dower to the raff,†
Swinging alone,
A solemn, tortured shadow in the air.

Fire!! (November 1926): 17.

*The base of an altarpiece.
†Trash or refuse.

Bottled

Upstairs, on the third floor
Of the 135th Street Library
In Harlem, I saw a little
Bottle of sand, brown sand,
Just like the kids make pies
Out of down at the beach.
But the label said: "This
Sand was taken from the Sahara desert."
Imagine that! The Sahara desert!
Some bozo's been all the way to Africa to get some sand.

And yesterday, on Seventh Avenue,
I saw a darky dressed fit to kill
In yellow gloves and swallow-tail coat
And swirling a cane. And everyone
Was laughing at him. Me too,
At first, till I saw his face
When he stopped to hear an
Organ grinder grind out some jazz.
Boy! You should a seen that darky's face!
It just shone. Gee, he was happy!
And he began to dance. No
Charleston or Black Bottom for *him*.
No sir. He danced just as dignified
And slow. No, not slow either,
Dignified and *proud!* You couldn't
Call it slow, not with all the
Steps he did. You would a died to see him.

Vanity Fair (May 1927): 76.
Caroling Dusk (1927): 221–23.

The crowd kept yellin' but he didn't hear,
Just kept on dancin' and twirling that cane,
And yellin' out loud every once in a while.

I know the crowd thought he was coo-coo.
But say, I was where I could see his face,
And somehow, I could see him dancin' in a jungle,
A real honest-to-cripe jungle, and he wouldn't have on
  them
Trick clothes—those yaller shoes and yaller gloves
And swallow-tail coat. He wouldn't have on nothing.
And he wouldn't be carrying no cane.
He'd be carrying a spear with a sharp fine point
Like the bayonets we had "over there":
And the end of it would be dipped in some kind of
Hoo-doo poison. And he'd be dancin', black and naked
  and gleaming.
And he'd have rings in his ears and on his nose,
And bracelets and necklaces of elephants' teeth.
Gee, I bet he'd be beautiful then, all right.
No one would laugh at him then, I bet.

Say! That boy that took that sand from the Sahara desert
And put it in a little bottle on a shelf in the library;
That's what they done to this shine, ain't it? Bottled him.

Those trick shoes, trick coat, trick cane, trick everything;
  all bottle;
But, *inside*—
Gee, that poor shine!

Poem

Little brown boy,
Slim, dark, big-eyed,
Crooning love songs to your banjo
Down at the Lafayette—*
Gee, boy, I love the way you hold your head,
High sort of and a bit to one side,
Like a prince, a jazz prince. And I love
Your eyes flashing, and your hands,
And your patent-leathered feet,
And your shoulders jerking the jig-wa.†
And I love your teeth flashing,
And the way your hair shines in the spotlight
Like it was the real stuff.
Gee, brown boy, I loves you all over.
I'm glad I'm a jig. I'm glad I can
Understand your dancin' and your
Singin', and feel all the happiness
And joy and don't-care in you.
Gee, boy, when you sing, I can close my ears
And hear tomtoms just as plain.
Listen to me, will you, what do I know
About tomtoms? But I like the word, sort of,
Don't you? It belongs to us.
Gee, boy, I love the way you hold your head,
And the way you sing and dance,

Caroling Dusk (1927): 218–19.
The Book of American Negro Poetry (1931): 279–81.

*Harlem's Lafayette Theater (1912–1964), located on Seventh Avenue near 131st Street.
†A lively dance.

And everything,
Say, I think you're wonderful. You're
All right with me,
You are.

Sonnet to a Negro in Harlem

You are disdainful and magnificent—
Your perfect body and your pompous gait,
Your dark eyes flashing solemnly with hate,
Small wonder that you are incompetent
To imitate those whom you so despise—
Your shoulders towering high above the throng,
Your head thrown back in rich, barbaric song,
Palm trees and mangoes stretched before your eyes.
Let others toil and sweat for labor's sake
And wring from grasping hands their meed* of gold.
Why urge ahead your supercilious feet?
Scorn will efface each footprint that you make.
I love your laughter arrogant and bold.
You are too splendid for this city street!

Caroling Dusk (1927): 217.
Ebony and Topaz (1927): 148.

*Reward or recompense.

Summer Matures

Summer matures. Brilliant Scorpion
Appears. The pelican's thick pouch
Hangs heavily with perch and slugs.
The brilliant-bellied newt flashes
Its crimson crest in the white water.
In the lush meadow, by the river,
The yellow-freckled toad laughs
With a toothless gurgle at the white-necked stork
Standing asleep on one red reedy leg.
And here Pan dreams of slim stalks clean for piping,
And of a nightingale gone mad with freedom.
Come. I shall weave a bed of reeds
And willow limbs and pale night flowers.
I shall strip the roses of their petals,
And the white down from the swan's neck.
Come. Night is here. The air is drunk
With wild grape and sweet clover.
And by the sacred fount of Aganippe
Euterpe sings of love. Ah, the woodland creatures,
The doves in pairs, the wild sow and her shoats,
The stag searching the forest for a mate,
Know more of love than you, my callous Phaon.*
The young moon is a curved white scimitar
Pierced through the swooning night.
Sweet Phaon. With Sappho sleep like the stars at dawn.
This night was born for love, my Phaon.
Come.

Opportunity (July 1927): 199.
Awarded Second Prize—Holstein Poetry Section.
Caroling Dusk (1927): 217–18.

*Alludes to the legend of Sappho's unconsummated love for Phaon.

What Do I Care for Morning

What do I care for morning,
For a shivering aspen tree,
For sunflowers and sumac
Opening greedily?
What do I care for morning,
For the glare of the rising sun,
For a sparrow's noisy prating,
For another day begun?
Give me the beauty of evening,
The cool consummation of night,
And the moon like a love-sick lady,
Listless and wan and white.
Give me a little valley,
Huddled beside a hill,
Like a monk in a monastery,
Safe and contented and still.
Give me the white road glistening,
A strand of the pale moon's hair,
And the tall hemlocks towering,
Dark as the moon is fair.
Oh what do I care for morning,
Naked and newly born—
Night is here, yielding and tender—
What do I care for dawn!

Caroling Dusk (1927): 216.

A Missionary Brings a Young Native to America

All day she heard the mad stampede of feet
Push by her in a thick unbroken haste.
A thousand unknown terrors of the street
Caught at her timid heart, and she could taste
The city grit upon her tongue. She felt
A steel-spiked wave of brick and light submerge
Her mind in cold immensity. A belt
Of alien tenets choked the songs that surged
Within her when alone each night she knelt
At prayer. And as the moon grew large and white
Above the roof, afraid that she would scream
Aloud her young abandon to the night,
She mumbled Latin litanies and dreamed
Unholy dreams while waiting for the light.

Harlem (November 1928): 40.

Cui Bono?*

She sat all day and thought of love.
She lay all night and dreamed it.
Our romance stricken little dove
Grew truly quite anaemic.

But one day Fate was satiate
Of her continuous pleading
And sent her down a passionate
Young knight to do her heeding.

And tho directly did she know
Their hearts were truly mated,
His eagerness she thought was so . . .
And so . . . she hesitated.

"If, if," she argued helplessly,
Alighting from his carriage
To hitch hike home respectably
"If he had offered marriage—"

"I wish I'd let him kiss me tho.
Oh, just the merest peck.
I wish—I wish—I wish, but no,
I'd lose my self-respect."

And so she sits and thinks of love.
And all night long she dreams it.
And with regret our little dove
Continues quite anaemic.

Harlem (November 1928): 11.

*Latin for "for whose benefit" or "of what good."

I Am Not Proud

I am not proud that I am bold
Or proud that I am black.
Color was given me as a gage
And boldness came with that.

The Saturday Evening Quill (April 1929): 75.

Invocation

Let me be buried in the rain
In a deep, dripping wood,
Under the warm wet breast of Earth
Where once a gnarled tree stood.
And paint a picture on my tomb
With dirt and a piece of bough
Of a girl and a boy beneath a round, ripe moon
Eating of love with an eager spoon
And vowing an eager vow.
And do not keep my plot mowed smooth
And clean as a spinster's bed,
But let the weed, the flower, the tree,
Riotous, rampant, wild and free,
Grow high above my head.

The Saturday Evening Quill (April 1929): 60.
The Book of American Negro Poetry (1931): 282.

Regalia

Stokin' stoves,
Emptin' garbage,
Fillin' ash cans,
Fixin' drain pipes,
Washin' stairs,
Answerin' a million calls,
Answerin' a million bells,
All day, half the night—
The yassuhs, the nosuhs,
The grins, the nods, the bowin'—
It sure wasn't no picnic
Bein' a janitor in a big apartment house in Harlem.
But, say, it was better than bein' back down home
Scrapin' to the buchra.* And he made good money, too,
With tips, now and then, for extra. His wife didn't have
To go out to do day's work any more, and Sammy, his only
  child,
Went to school and learned readin' and writin'. And he,
Big Sam, had been able to join the local lodge.
He would have rather gone without his vittles
Than not pay his lodge dues,
Than not march in the lodge parade,
Than not wear his uniform of blue and gold and orange,
And high white plumes and yellow braid and gold
  epaulets,
And snow-white gloves and shining black shoes and
  tassels,

The Saturday Evening Quill (April 1929): 14–15.

*The boss man.

And silk ribbons and feathers and big bright buttons and
Color, color, color.
God, how he loved it! He loved it better than food and
drink,—
Better than Love itself.
Every night after work, after
The stove stokin'
The garbage slingin',
The ashcan fillin',
The stair washin',
The yassuhs and nosuhs and the grins and nods and
bowin',
He'd go downstairs to his basement flat and put it on.
And stand in front of his crazy old mirror and make funny
Gestures and military signs and talk to himself and click
His heels together and curse and swear like a major or a
General. And always he'd be the leader, the head, and
The others, the make-believe others, would say yassuh
and nosuh,
And grin and nod and bow. Gold and yellow and blue—
God, how he loved it!

That old Rev. Giddings was a fool, telling him it was a sin
To dress up and have music and march when somebody
died.
"God don't like that," he said. "God, He wants mourning
And wailing and dark clothes. He don't want all that
worldly
Music and color for his dead children. He don't want all
that
Regalia. It hurts Him, Brother, it hurts Him. It's vanity,

That's all. You don't know, Brother, that blue and gold
You wear—the flames of Hell; that red—the blood of His
Crucified Son, those plumes and feathers—they mocked
Christ
With them once. God don't like that regalia, son. God
don't
Like it. I got to stay in the lodge or I'd lose my flock.
You know that, Brother. But dress in black when I die,
Brother,
And beat your breast. I don't want no regalia."
But Sam couldn't understand. He loved it so, that uniform.
What had it to do with God?
Nights when the lodge went on parade. Nights when
there was
A funeral and they had to march in a long, beautiful
procession.
His wife was proud of him, and so was Sammy, his son,
Who wanted to be a general in the army.
If only there might be a funeral . . .

And then one night Rev. Giddings died
And Sam had a chance to wear his uniform—
His uniform of blue and gold and orange—
And high white plumes and yellow braid and gold
epaulets,
And snow-white gloves and shining black shoes and
tassels,
And silk ribbons and feathers and big bright buttons,
And color, color, color.
But it was different. Reverend Giddings must have
conjured him.

He was scared. His plumes bent him over and the color
before
Him was like Hell fire. And there was Rev. Giddings
Smiling at him. "God don't like all that regalia, Brother,
God don't like it." The blue and gold flames leaped up
And burned him. Red swarmed before him, banners,
Ribbons. He saw strips of blood, streams of blood flowing
About him—"The blood of His Crucified Son." And the
music,
The drums, the bugles—The little red devils dancing
before
His eyes—The flames lapping up the blood—Red, blue,
gold.
God, how he hated it!
He snatched off his plumes, tore off his colors, beat his
breast.

It was hard to make him out in all that flood of color.
He seemed so little and tired and bent and dark and
humble.
He looked so funny, beating his breast that way.
In fact, he looked more like the little colored janitor
Who stoked stoves,
And emptied garbage,
And piled ashcans,
And scrubbed stairs
In a big apartment house in Harlem,
Than anything else.

Remember Not

Remember not the promises we made
In this same garden many moons ago.
You must forget them. I would have it so.
Old vows are like old flowers as they fade
And vaguely vanish in a feeble death.
There is no reason why your hands should clutch
At pretty yesterdays. There is not much
Of beauty in me now. And though my breath
Is quick, my body sentient, my heart
Attuned to romance as before, you must
Not, through mistaken chivalry, pretend
To love me still. There is no mortal art
Can overcome Time's deep, corroding rust.
Let Love's beginning expiate Love's end.

The Saturday Evening Quill (April 1929): 76.
The Book of American Negro Poetry (1931): 282.

Rustic Fantasy

The goat's milk is sweeter.
The white bellied frog
Forsakes the water and its tail for land.
The wild sow and her shoats
Make defloration of the forest fruits.
A roebuck leads a troop of fallow deer
To a fragrant field of clover.
Despite the marten,*
The mole ejects her young,
Is anchoret† again in snug seclusion.
Hermes rests beneath the cool shade of a date tree
His lips thirsty for an open gourd.
The bees are warm with honey . . .

The Saturday Evening Quill (April 1929): 23.

*A small, furry animal.
†A hermit.

Why Do They Prate?

Why do they prate of youth so much?
'Tis too near the root.
A budding, yes, but I prefer
The ripening of the fruit.

The Saturday Evening Quill (April 1929): 60.

Worship

I want to worship God,
And so I go to church. There is a church two blocks down
Between the baker's and the new hospital.
I enter and kneel down on the prayer mat to pray.
But no prayer comes. I am not good. I am a sinner.
I am alone in the House of God and cannot think of God.
It is so strange in here, and close and dead.
I will not stay any longer. I will not wait any longer for
God.

I draw on my glove and rush out into the street.
There! I am free. Here is Beauty, cold, white, clean.
Soft snow wets my cheeks. I want to worship God.
Is not this devotion? Is not this worship?
I worship God's gift, Nature:
Do I not thus worship Him—the Giver?

I pass a beggar woman and empty my purse in her lap.
Her eyes grow bright. There is a sort of worship in her
eyes—
"Beautiful gold—smooth, warm, beautiful."
She polishes the money with her breath. I leave her there
Worshipping my gift, gold, with no thought for me, the
Giver.

The trees are like white holyroods, wind-riven,
As I turn and blindly make my way back to the church.
I want to worship God.

The Saturday Evening Quill (April 1929): 21.

Vers de Societe

And if I was mistaken—
If your fealty is glossed,
If all your vows were taken
With every finger crossed—

Later I shall be wary,
But later I shall be old.
There is no time to tarry
Since only the young are bold.

Love's an omelette, rum sprinkled,
Set on fire and served while hot,
Puffed to a heavenly fragrance,
Light as a pollen dot.

Be careful it does not fall, dear.
Make haste and have your meal.
Only the dotard is prudent.
Only the dead are leal.*

Opportunity (July 1930): 210.

*Loyal, faithful, honest, and true.

Sonnet [Be not averse to Beauty]

Be not averse to Beauty or to love.
Entreat them in your daily prayer and song.
Make them your truth and know the peace thereof,
And they will nourish you, sweetly, and long.
Ah, let your swaddled psychic strength unfold,
Grow in awareness, delicate and keen.
But keep the tingleness of life and mold
Your way in Beauty, vigorous and clean.
Believe in things; all living is belief.
The doubting heart when hungry must be fed;
And freely, for the meal is fine, tho brief,
Beauty's the wine, and Love the loaf of bread.
They are the sacrament of Life I think,
So eat your warm white bread and drink and drink.

Opportunity (December 1931): 374.

Sonnet [Wisdom May Caution]

Your dark head lies complacent on my breast.
Your lovely mouth is satiate. I fear
You know me far too well. Your childlike rest
Reflects my placid constancy too clear.
Of late even my thoughts are not my own.
You hum the tune I'm humming in my mind.
You know me thoroughly, flesh to the bone.

Therefore, think me not utterly so blind
That I heed not that you have been untrue,
That soon you will forsake me, leave me bare,
Will pity me for ever trusting you,
The while you learn that other arms are fair.
But what avails it to foretell the end?
Wisdom may caution, but it will not mend.

Opportunity (March 1932): 81.

Monotone

My life is but a single attitude,
An endless preface,
An old day-by-day.
My soul is a slack gesture of content—
Plump eiderdown piled high upon the bed
My mind is like a scene in pastels that
A careful child paints on a china plate;
Precisely pretty, if impersonal;—
But half conceived, yet not inadequate.

Opportunity (September 1932): 286.

Widow with a Moral Obligation

Won't you come again, my friend?
I'll not be so shy.
I shall have a candle lit
To light you by.
I shall have my hair unbound,
My gown undone,
And we shall have a night of love
And death in one.
I was very foolish
To have run away before,
But you see I thought I heard
Him knocking at the door,
But you see I thought I saw
Him smiling in your smile,
And I saw his lips call
Me something very vile.
It must have been my conscience
Or a quirk in my head,
For I knew he'd been
A long time dead.
We buried him one morning
In the sweet cool rain.
But when you come tonight,
We must bury him again.
You must come and rid me
Of my dear leal wraith.
We can bury him so easy
When he's lost his faith.
Stab with little poniards—

Challenge (March 1934): 38.

Every kiss will be a knife.
And we will be cruel,
For life is life.
Ah come again, my friend,
I'll not be so shy.
I shall have a candle lit
To light you by.
I shall have my hair unbound,
My gown undone,
And we shall have a night of love
And death in one.

Plea of a Plebeian

I'd like to be a lady. Gee—
A lady with a pedigree—
With haughty airs and careless grace.
Nobility writ on my face.
    The peasant class is very well,
    But I like something awfully swell.

I strongly wish my blood were blue.
Think of the things that I could do.
Think of the places I could go
If I were Lady So-and-So.
    And in my elegant salon
    I could make charming liaisons.

A gallant in both word and deed
Would bear me on his handsome steed
To some romantic palisade
For an historic escapade.
    The middle class has quite a pull,
    But they are so respectable.

I could be either fat or slight
(A lady bows to appetite).
And I could wear my last year's hat.
Or the chapeau prior to that
    And still inspire gallantry,
    Were I a dame of pedigree.

Opportunity (May 1934): 144.

Let Me Sing My Song

Let me sing my song,
Let me speak my piece.
Let the little soul of me find release
In the pounding rain
And the sucking mud;
The prehensible earth,
The salt of blood;
In the hungry moon,
The bleating night;
The moulded hill—
Dawn's acolyte;
In the level eyes
And the clasp of friends;
The plump little pool
Where the thin stream ends;
The germinal gleam
Groping, untaught,
Flexing the cramped mind
In thought;
Love flowing east,
Love flowing west—
The level land;
The mountain's breasts;
Let me sing my song,
Let me speak my piece.
Let the little soul of me find release
In the tree's roots,
The flower's breath.—
I fear the barren drought of death.

Challenge (May 1935): 44.

Goin' No'th

"Goodbye, mammy, at de cabin do'
Goin' no'th, won't see you no mo.' "

Good tune to dat song alright,
But de words was jes' a mess of lies.
He was goin' no'th, leavin' mammy and pappy and Lena,
But he'd be sendin' back fo' dem soon
And den dey'd all come no'th and live in a big house
Lak Missus' on de hill.
It was goin' be easy findin' work up no'th
Where you could pick money off de streets.
Everybody told him to git up no'th
And make somethin' of hisself. He was too smart
To stay down south pickin' cotton—
Allus jes' pickin' cotton.

Mammy'd done give him a silk handkerchief.
He'd never had nothin' silk before. She musta saved
And saved to bought it. And it sure looked good
Stickin' so every-day like out of his top pocket. Looked
lots different
Den de red cotton cloth he always carried.

Pappy had give him a small pocket Bible.
He was goin' need dat, alright. Ev'y man had to have de
Word of God wid him when he was travellin' or he
wouldn't
Have no luck. It was nice to feel it thump in his pants
Pocket when he walked. And in his other pocket was his
wallet

(Previously unpublished.)

Wid his money and ticket in it safe and solid.
Dere he was, de happies man in de world, wid his God
In one pocket and his money in de other pocket,
Walkin' along just lak one o' de buchra.

Wonder what de girls was goin' be lak up no'th?
He didn't care if dey was pretty as de stars or
Ugly as de conjur women. He was goin' send fo' Lena
 anyway
Directly he got settled. In de lapel of his coat
Was a little bunch of flowers Lena had give him dis
Mo'nin'. He'd promised her to keep dem forever,
And dat was a promise he sure was goin' keep. Lena
Wid her black eyes and soft woolly hair and her skin
Dark and cool as de summer night is after de lightnin'
 flashes.

Better shift his grip a little.
Had to hurry a mite now. Dat train was mos' due
'Roun' de bend. . . . Splash!
Right in de middle of a puddle left from last night's rain.
Brand new yeller shoes all spattered and messed up!
Dis sure was a nice to-do. He had to scrub de mud off 'em
Some way. Phew! Dat was a job! And there was somethin'
 soft
Dragging under one of his boots—Lena's flowers!
Lord today! Dey musta fell from his lapel while he was
Bendin' over cleanin' his boots. And he'd messed dem up
In de mud! And Gawd-Almighty, he'd clean forgot dat
Was the silk handkerchief 'stead of his usual red cotton
Cloth in his upper pocket—
And he done used it to clean his shoes with!

Lord, dey'd cry dere eyes out if dey knew
'Bout dis. Po' mammy and Lena. Po' him.
He wouldn't have no luck up no'th at all now.
What was he goin' do? He couldn' leave mammy's
Silk handkerchief all torn and black out dere in de road.
And here was de train comin'. He could hear it grumblin'
Over de bend and wouldn' be long now befo' it'd be
Snortin' up to de station. He'd have to run to make it
Fo' sure. What he goin' do 'bout dese things?
He'd never in dis world have no luck if he lef' dem
Dere in de road for de cows to tramp over and all.
He could put dem in his valise, messy and soggy wid
Mud as dey was only if he ever opened dat bag out dere
In de road he'd have a time gettin' it together again.
It was stuffed mos' to burstin' wid his clothes and
Bed linen and mammy's fried chicken.
And dere was his train in sight!

Lord, how he was runnin'! Dese yeller shoes
Musta had wings on dem. Here was de train 'long side of it,
A leap—somethin' solid like Droppin' from his pocket on
De track? But he was on de train now, goin' no'th.
What was dat dropped, though? His wallet! Wid his money
And his ticket in it! Man, what he goin' do now.
On bo'd de train no'th wid no money and no ticket.
Lord, warn't he goin' no'th after all?

Wait a minute—Here was de wallet.
Jus' as safe. He sure was a fool. Dat musta bin de
Bible his pappy had give him dis mo'nin dat fall on de
track.
Lord! Dat sure was a narrow escape, alright.

'Course he'd buy another Bible directly he got no'th.
No'th. Goin' No'th. Goin' No'th at las', Lord.

"Goodbye, mammy, at de cabin do'
Goin' no'th, won't see you no mo'."

Good tune to dat song alright, But de words
Was jes' a mess of lies.

Rootbound

Heavy shovels
Boiling soapsuds
Opening cab doors
Washing cuspidors
Running numbers
Selling "hot goods"
Dodging cops—
He was tired of Harlem
Tired of New York
Tired of America—
Somebody always calling you nigger
Always keeping you down
Always joking 'bout your color.
A man couldn't have no pride
And stay in a country like this.
They didn't want him here
And he sure didn't have to stay
Where he wasn't wanted.
Not now.
He had money saved up—
Most a thousand dollars
And he was going to leave this white man's country for
    good.
That's why he's at the harbor. His luggage aboard.
His ticket in his wallet.
All set.
Almost. Almost.

(Previously unpublished.)

The American flag at the harbor rippled in the breeze.
What did that mean to him
Or to his mammy and pappy who'd worked and fought their way up North
So he could be brung up like a man.
Like a man.
Would a man run away from things?
His people, all those strong patient black people—
They'd fought for this country, worked hard on it
They'd been hung and burned on it, too.
But they'd stuck. They didn't run.
After all, only white folks get scared,
Kill themselves, run away from things.
Not cullud folks, has guts.
He wasn' letting no white trash chase him from his home.

The American flag at the harbor fluttered in the breeze.
Defiantly he took off his cap.
His straightened black hair shone like patent leather in the sun,
But it was really very kinky at the roots.

Foraging

I cannot go on living in this very little way—
This tea, this bread and butter set so neatly on a tray.
If I close the door behind me, careful not to let it slam
I might sneak out and get myself a little bit of jam.

(Previously unpublished.)

He's About 22. I'm 63.*

He's About 22. I'm 63.
A pity! He's so pretty!
He runs up the stairs.
I climb step by step.
We've never really met, and yet
if I could stop him, what could I say?
"How's my young man today?"
Absurd! He'd give the sweet unspecial smile
You give a sweet unspecial child.
At most, some gingham word.

He's slightly effete, completely elite,
his grace unsurpassed, a young prince at mass.
My cardiac wheezing is frantic and panting.
He's enchanting!

Why was he born so late,
And I so soon?
A turn of chance
the nearest happenstance,
but move, if you're *that*
upset.

Then I won't know if I fit,
whether to sit back and
sit, or quit altogether.
To wit:

*The remaining poems are among those written from the early 1960s to the early 1980s, when Johnson, then past age fifty, lived on Thompson Street in Greenwich Village.

Do I have it, or is it gone?
Do I still belong? Can I bluff?
Suppose he turns schoolboy-tough?
Oh, it's all too much!

Look, get his name from the mailbox
and see if he's in the book.

Well, it won't hurt to look.
Here it is.

Then phone. If he's divine,
he's probably at home, a "want-to-be
alone."

My God, he *is* home!
6D?   6C.

I'm so sorry but my zipper's caught,
with my hair in it.

Yes, it *is* ridiculous,
but *would* you? For just a minute?

Come in. The door's unlocked.
God! He glows! And even younger
than I thought.

You knew all that before.
You're becoming a bore.

But how can I reach him?

Teach him, then beseech him.

He seems a little scattered.

How does it really matter? at 22, at 63,
any eccentricity?

But will it all be left to me?
Certainly.
That's the idea.
Breathe heavily
(asthma with rhythm)

You mean, a mini-cataclysm?

Yes. More or less.
Relax. It isn't worth the
sweat. Don't forget, it's
luck, not skill.

He's virile?

Puerile.

How droll.
But better droll than
cold, and no reason for
distress. Last night
you had far less.

You're right.
Last night the futile victory
  the lonely ecstasy
  the peakless summit
  the remote spasm
  the chasm, the gap,
  the hi without the ho.

Tonight I might not touch the sky
but I'll be on tippy-toe.

So,
burgeoning 22,
ripening 63,
enjoy your buoyancy.
Whisper triumphantly,
"Merci, Merci."

(Or less jubilantly,
"Mercy!")

A Moment of Dignity

Give me a moment of dignity
of pragmatic worth—
a tie, a laundered shirt,
a taxi signal flourish,
before I nestle pleasantly
into the rubbish.

Time After Time

Time after time
there is a
Once upon a time.

Old woman
waiting for the bus
nervous in the sliced line
fumbling your ID card, listening hard to
some inner, meager bard.

Someone will stand, steady your hand
                                        "Thank you so much."
                                        "Not at all, ma'm."

Their eyes do not see you. You understand.
They subscribe to the alive, the me-toos,
      the withs, the next, the flexible.

You are invisible to the dimensioned.

You've become petulant. The tea is never right.

At night, the lack, the looking back, the
      constant reminiscence wrinkling the
      brow of now, the defensive rigidness,
      the blinkless stare, the tired
      decisions and revisions

Where did forgiveness go, the gentleness,
      the warm and generous "Hello"

"We'll have tea
and day-old
cinnamon buns.
Do come."

It need not be that way, old woman.

Skip the lonely flicks. Mix. Tremble the air! Resemble!
Declare! Inhale! Exhale! Blare! Blare loudly! Louder than
the crowd!!!

Ignore the meek. They have no fervor.
They die from murmured violence, littered silences.
They die at ends of queues, mewing, waiting, waiting in
good faith,
unembittered.

Time is a roll of dimes bought at the carnival.
Dimes for winds.
No free winds.
Each wind a dime.

Wind the wheels of chance.
Wind the little porno films and the belly dolls that dance.
Wind the wax soothsayer, and the imprinted prayers.
Wind until the springs break.

Catch the sweet cascade, prepaid, mechanically made,
the nectar and ambrosia,
the syrupy nostalgia.
the orangeade,

the grapeade
the lemonade
the limeade
Drink up! Crush the paper cup and
let it quiver to the floor.

Old woman
Gulp the joy!
Belch the pity!
Straddle the city!

War

War is delectable
the blood
the shredded limb
the belly, yielding grace
guts funnily displace.

War is delicious
the rot
the feeling in the severed hand
the fulfilled command

Stir the pulverized face
the film
the stale urine
the seminal waste

Trace your fiscal logo.
It's there, somewhere.

War—Part II

More? More of the same?
Yes. More of the same.

War is extravagant
lavish
dear.

Tomorrow's vineyard clinically coffined
and dated
and rated
an excellent year.

Votre sante!
Salud!
Ole!

The Street to the Establishment

You're the old. I'm the new
I'm the multi. You're the few
You're the gained, the attained,
the begun, the become,
the prize that's been won
the picked from the which.
You're part of the mural on the wall,
the spire that cannot fall.
I'm the aborted
I'm the itch.

For Jason

Little boys are so pleasant
Why not love them as they are?
Cheer their jousts. Shine their armor
Know their wonder,
Share their star.

They are not far below us.
Why can't we kneel a bit?
See what they try to show us.
Sit in reverent surprise.

Are we afraid of the reflection in their eyes?

A Boy Like Me

First boy

I wish I had a boy like me, debonair, with
longish hair, able to fit into our cradle.

We should be very much aware, the first
night
in his little lair, that love and valor placed
him there unlabeled. Please take this very
seriously. I want a boy deliciously like me.

Second boy

I'd hold him all day in my arms and sing
schematic little songs. He'd never grow
up
muscle-bound cerebrally, but free and
strong
with double charm and alternate
propensities.

First boy

To have a charming bit of chap
completely helpless
in my lap, and take his condescending nap
against my chest, or breast. Shamelessly
and foolhardy, and I hope irregardlessly, I
want a little boy like me.

A boy like me would be so sweet I'd eat
him
with a spoon. I'd teach him how to say a
prayer
to Love, to God, and not to care if he is
not
the president, or next man on the moon.

Second boy
To compose a boy like you there must be
fused identities:
you
me
a neutered muse
No scientific ruse.

To the ordinaries:
Groping beneath covers for new hues.
You
concepts of concession and dittoed
thought,
pass the baptismal bowl. But if no cowled
blessing, steal a wino blessing from a
paper
bag of naughts and tangled souls.
and
Anoint us.

Now, to the established clergy:
Christen us with certitudes
attitudes
fat little platitudes
ahas, ahems
strategems
carefully cued amens.

Pardon.
From now on either boy may spout his own mouthful
of jargon.

Everything is wondrous, synonymous, reverent and
irreverent,

a quandary of geo-mores, becauses:

I love you because
I don't love you
because
I can't love you
because.

Love conceives. The eternal strength of love is love conceives. To evolve a fitting little boy, a composite, witty little boy, we must revolve in innocence, benevolent intent. Love is the ultimate event, the embraced extent, the Signature, the unframed becoming the became.

Everything is once upon a time
Everything can rhyme, flow
Everything that breathes conceives

Simply reason
Simply believe
Simply *know.*

We could have a little boy like me so easily, easy as spit.
We fit.

Then let's have it—

not a rare, symbolic little boy
but a colicky, burping, belching
little boy
as real as porridge.

Dear God, don't
bother to be horrified or sorry.
Be whole, entire,
    undiminished.

Please,   God, the Father,
    May I be a mother, too,
    like you? made in your image?

The Whimsy of It All

A little room at the end of a hall,
A chair, a bed. The room is small.
And faintly smudged on the blistered wall—
"I love you."

Why do I come back?
To be enthralled
by ghosts grown tall?
Or to enjoy the whimsy of it all?

The Quest

When you are old you become singular and dry
When you are old you stop asking why.
You always know.

So

If the quest is stilled
and the full circle is a vise,
how circumspect,
how elegant,
to genuflect (or curtsy), and to die.

Helene Johnson, 1931

All photos: Schlesinger Library, Radcliffe Institute, Harvard University

above

First cousins Helene Johnson, Dorothy West, Eugenia Rickson, and friend, Lois Mailou Jones

right

Helene Johnson, about twelve years old

opposite

Helene Johnson, about seventeen years old

Dorothy West, Oak Bluffs

opposite, above

Dorothy West, New York City

opposite, below

Gay Head, Massachusetts. Eugenia Rickson (wearing the cross), Dorothy West (with the headwrap), and Marian Minus (directly behind West).

Helene Johnson and her daughter

opposite

Helene Johnson and Dorothy West

H. J.
D. W.

Dorothy West, Martha's Vineyard, 1995

Helene Johnson

A Chronology

EDITOR'S NOTE: *As Cheryl Wall writes in the foreword, Helene Johnson strenuously guarded her private life and largely succeeded in placing a veil over it. I offer "A Chronology" and "Selected Letters," then, to begin to lift that veil. To the extent that they shed light on her life, the chronology and letters help us to contextualize and thereby more fully understand Johnson's poetry. The letters span the period 1927 (when Johnson was age twenty-one and recently arrived in New York City) to 1948 (when forty-two-year-old Johnson was residing in Brooklyn with her husband, mother, and daughter). What emerges from these letters is a beautiful portrait of one who was simultaneously hard-working, playful, shy, witty, and (as she reveals in a 1932 letter to West) in love: "I've been in love again and you know what that means to me. I'm normal again now, tho, darling."*

These letters have particular importance in that they shed light on an intimate "literary community," composed of Helene Johnson, Dorothy West, and Zora Neale Hurston. We receive a vivid portrait of the trio's close friendship and warmly affirmative support for each others' writings. Not only did they encourage each other, but they met and as Hurston notes, "worked out" ideas.

Where possible and necessary, I provide explanatory notes on persons mentioned in the letters. Johnson, West, Hurston, Rachel West, Abigail Hubbell, and Wallace Thurman appear most prominently. Rachel West was Dorothy West's mother and Helene Johnson's aunt. Abigail Hubbell is Helene Johnson's daughter. Wallace Thurman (1902–1934) was, with the possible exception of Hurston, the cousins' closest friend in Harlem's intellectual circle. He published three novels and edited two short-lived literary journals, Fire!! A Quarterly Devoted to the Younger Negro Artists *(1926) and* Harlem: A Forum of Negro Life *(1928). Johnson contributed two poems to* Harlem *and one to* Fire!!

7 July 1906: Born Helen Virginia Johnson in Boston's New England Women's Hospital. The only child of George William Johnson, of Nashville, Tennessee, and Ella Benson Johnson of Camden, South Carolina.

2 June 1907: Dorothy West, Johnson's maternal first cousin, born in Boston to Rachel Pease Benson West and Isaac Christopher West.

1910: Johnson and West grow up together, initially at 30 Cedar Street, in Boston's Roxbury section. Also living with them is their maternal Aunt Minnie Rickson and her daughter Eugenia, known as Jean.

1911: The three young cousins take piano lessons and are tutored at home by Maude Trotter Steward and Bessie Trotter Craft, daughters of William Monroe Trotter (1872–1934), founding editor of the influential *Boston Guardian*. A few of Johnson's early poems appear in the *Boston Guardian*.

1911: The cousins spend their childhood summers in the village of Oak Bluffs, on Martha's Vineyard Island. Next door to their family's cottage is the family cottage of the cousins' friend, the visual artist and longtime Howard University Professor Lois Mailou Jones.

1911–1923: Johnson attends public schools in Boston: the Lafayette School, the Martin School in the Mission Hill District, and Girls' Latin High School.

1913: The family moves to 45 Clifford Street, Roxbury.

1914: The family moves to a four-storied house at 478 Brookline Avenue, a few miles south of Boston University and a five-minute walk from the present Brigham and Women's Hospital.

1923: Johnson takes courses at Boston Clerical School and at Boston University.

1925: Johnson and West join The Saturday Evening Quill Club, an organization of aspiring black Boston writers. Meetings are held at the Cambridge home of Club President Eugene Gordon and his wife Edythe.

1925: Johnson's short story "Respectability" wins first prize in a literary contest sponsored by the black-owned *Boston Chronicle*, which publishes it.

May 1925: "Trees at Night," published in the National Urban League's journal *Opportunity*, brings Johnson national attention.

1926: In Braithwaite's *Anthology of Magazine Verse*, Johnson lists theater, tennis, dancing, hiking, and rowing as her recreations; Whitman, Tennyson, Shelley, and Sandburg are her favorite poets.

April 1926: West and Johnson travel to New York City for *Opportunity*'s Second Annual Literary Awards Dinner, held at the Fifth Avenue Restaurant on May 1. Johnson's poems win three honorable mentions and West shares the second-place prize for fiction with Zora Neale Hurston.

January 1927: Johnson and West move to New York City.

February 1927: Hurston leaves New York City for central Florida to conduct research. Johnson and West study journalism at Columbia University.

May 1927: Johnson publishes "Bottled" in *Vanity Fair* to wide acclaim. Hurston writes from Florida, offering Johnson and West her New York City apartment.

June 1927: Johnson and West accept Hurston's offer and move from the 137th Street YWCA to Hurston's 43 West 66th Street apartment, the only apartment building in mid-Manhattan that accepts blacks.

June 1928: The Saturday Evening Quill Club publishes its first annual, *The Saturday Evening Quill*.

March 1929: West travels to London as part of the cast of *Porgy*. Johnson visits Detroit with Wallace Thurman.

29 October 1929: The stock market collapses, bringing on the Great Depression, which hastens the end of the Harlem Renaissance.

1930: Johnson works for Hurston, most likely typing and conducting research.

14 February 1931: In a letter to Langston Hughes, Hurston writes, "Helene Johnson is in the hospital now having her tonsils out and I think I shall do the same before warm weather."

15 June 1932: West travels to Russia with Langston Hughes and 18 other black intellectuals to film *Black and White*, a movie about life in black America. Beset by controversy, the film is never completed.

1933: West's father dies, and she returns from Russia to her mother's home at 23 Worthington Street, Boston. Johnson marries William Warner Hubbell III, a New York City motorman.

1934–1937: West founds and edits *Challenge* and *New Challenge*.

22 December 1934: Wallace Thurman dies in New York City. "For me," says West, "Wally's death meant the end of the Harlem Renaissance."

May 1935: Johnson's last published poem, "Let Me Sing My Song," appears in *Challenge*, volume 1.3.

March 1937: Back from the West Indies, where she finished writing *Their Eyes Were Watching God*, an elated Hurston invites West and Johnson to her Seventh Avenue apartment.

18 September 1940: Johnson's only child, Abigail Calachaly Hubbell, is born in New York City.

1945: West leaves New York City for Martha's Vineyard, where she lives the remainder of her life.

1948: Johnson lives with her husband, mother, and daughter at 81 North Portland Avenue, Brooklyn, New York. West publishes *The Living Is Easy*. Hurston publishes *Seraph on the Suwanee*.

1940s–1950s: Johnson works as a correspondent for Consumers Union in Mount Vernon, New York. The Harlem Renaissance poet Gwendolyn Bennett also works there as a correspondent.

early 1960s–early 1980s: Johnson lives at 210 Thompson Street in Greenwich Village.

28 January 1960: Hurston dies in Saint Lucie County, Florida.

c. 1962: Johnson's daughter, Abigail, a theater major, graduates from Bard College.

December 1962: Johnson writes to Arna Bontemps, granting him permission to publish four of her poems in his anthology *American Negro Poetry.*

December 1971: Johnson travels to London and Paris with her daughter, son-in-law, and grandsons.

early 1980s: Johnson leaves New York City and lives for a few years in Onset, Massachusetts.

1986: Increasingly afflicted by osteoporosis, Johnson returns to New York City.

8 February 1987: A poetry reading at Manhattan's Off Center Theater, 436 West 18th Street, features a recording of Johnson reciting her poems.

1993: Lois Mailou Jones's *Breezy Day at Gay Head,* selected by President Clinton, becomes the first painting by an African American to hang in the White House.

1995: West publishes *The Wedding.* The novel's heroine is modeled loosely on Johnson's daughter, Abigail.

6 July 1995: Johnson dies the day before her eighty-ninth birthday, at her daughter's Manhattan home.

16 August 1998: West dies in Boston at age ninety-one.

July 1999: Eugenia Rickson, the last of the three cousins, dies in New York City at age ninety-two.

Selected Letters

From: Zora Neale Hurston, General Delivery, Sanford, Florida
To: Dorothy West and Helene Johnson, 137th Street YWCA[?], NYC

[Sunday] 22 May 1927

Dear Little Sisters D & H—
Yes, I'm married now, Mrs. Herbert Arnold Sheen, if you please.* He is in his last year at the U. of Chicago Med. School, but is going to stay out until we get a good start. We are all quite happy now. But write me still by my maiden name as I don't want my mail balled up.

Darlings, see can you find me a copy of Elmer Gantry. I am submerged down here in this wilderness, where such books are not for sale.

Things going dull down here. Working hard, but the people are impossible—all except my husband. The scenery is gorgeous, though.

I have given up writing things until the expedition is over. Then I shall try again. By the way, I hope you two ran away with the "O" contest. I *know* you did even though I have heard nor seen a thing down here in the swamps.

Tired and full of indigestion so I shall not write at length. My love to all the bunch.

Lovingly your sister, Zora

P.S. Do you girls want my apartment for 3 months? You can keep it cheaper than you can your present quarters besides greater comfort insured. I shall not return until Sept & by that time, I might be able to get a front apartment and let you keep it, having a hubby to look out for me, now.

Any way, let me hear from you at once as I know several

*Hurston and Sheen were married in St. Augustine, Florida, on 19 May 1927. See Robert Hemenway's *Zora Neale Hurston: A Literary Biography* (Champaign: University of Illinois Press, 1977).

people who want it, and I cannot afford to keep it vacant. The man who had it is ill in Chicago, and had to give it up.

Lovingly
Zora

From: Zora Neale Hurston, Box 5201, Sta. B, New Orleans
To: Dorothy West and Helene Johnson, 43 W. 66th St.,
2nd floor rear (?), NYC

[Thursday] 22 Nov 1928

Dear My Children,
Thanks for your favors. Look for a parcel for yourselves in a day or two. Don't look for coherence in this letter. I am merely trying to get it said.

Things going fine. Have a brilliant new idea to work out, hence my request for the material. Sure you will be thrilled. Bully for the new magazine,* shall hurry home to do what I can. Got lots of things for you to help me work out as soon as I get there.

My love to all the folks, no I guess you better not say anything.

Shall see perhaps sooner than I had anticipated.

Luck and love,
Zora

*Wallace Thurman's *Harlem, A Forum of Negro Life* (November 1928).

From: Zora Neale Hurston, New Orleans

To: Dorothy West, 43 W. 66th St., 2nd floor rear (?), NYC

Wednesday, 5 Dec 1928

Dear Dot Child,

If I gave you the idea I was coming home soon it was during one of my trance periods.* I wont be home for months & when I *do*, it will be so sketchy that you can just stick me on the day-bed. I'll be in & out of town so I probably wont need any apartment.

Did you get the box of pecans I sent you for Thanksgiving?

Love to my Helene

Zora

Same P.O. address

Wish I could help out on "Harlem" but it is impossible at present. I'm heartbroken over being bound to silence. Are you tired of the place?

*Hurston spent the winter of 1928–1929 in New Orleans studying hoodoo and experiencing firsthand trances and other psychic phenomena. She details these experiences in *Mules and Men* (Philadelphia: Lippincott, 1935).

From: Dorothy West, London
To: Rachel West, 470 Brookline Ave., Boston

Sunday [19 May 1929]

Dearest Mother,
I do hope by now that one of you has heard from Helene. She has not written to me which does seem strange, but I trust she is well and not unhappy. "Porgy" closes the 25th of May, and we do not yet know whether we go on to the continent or return home. I shall let you know the minute I learn. "Porgy" has been only an artistic success, and a financial disappointment.

I think I will wait a bit before I write to the publishers, as I am uncertain where I shall be to receive their answer. I am glad you like Louise. I will try to bring her a little gift.

I am quite at home in London now, and shall be sorry to leave. I have given much and learned much in the weeks I have been here. There is nothing so broadening as travel. Every day I realize that.

I am having a great deal of fun with Countée,* and shall be sorry to leave him. He is staying on until the last of June, and then going back to Paris.

We had a nice lunch with a Miss Otto this afternoon with a butler to serve us, and afterwards we went to the birthday party of one of the members of our company, and I met many well-known colored actors, among them George Dewey Washington whom you may have heard on the Vitaphone.

Tomorrow Ed and I are going to see a beautiful play, "Journey's End," which is also running in New York. Incidentally I saw Mary Pickford in "Coquette" and liked neither. Tuesday Ed and Countée are inviting me to the dinner that Ed is to cook, Wednesday we are going to an informal

*The Harlem Renaissance poet Countee Cullen (1903–1946).

gathering at the home of a nice Englishwoman, who has a [?] ship, whom we met at Miss Otto's. Thursday Emma Leighton, Bertha Corton's very grand sister, who has one of the loveliest houses in London, is giving an affair, and we are going out after the theater. I expect I will dress for that. And Sunday, for the first time, I am going to John Payne's where everyone goes at least once while in London.

Continue to write me until the 25th, and I shall probably be in London a week longer, either waiting for the boat to sail or waiting to go on to Berlin.

Lots of love,
Dot

From: Wallace Thurman, 308 E. 9th South St., Salt Lake City
To: Dorothy West and Helene Johnson, Oak Bluffs, Massachusetts

Friday [30 August 1929]

Dear Dot and Helene:

It is measly writing you a single note for two, but I have been quite ill for the past month, and am now in no mood to write or even think consecutive or coherent thoughts.

I am worried about you Helene. The leg? How on earth did it happen? Is that all Harlem could do for you?

And Dot, so cosmopolitan now. A traveled lady planning to spend the winter in Paris. The idea of a colony intrigues me although such things generally turn out to be stupid unless colorful personality abounds, and then it grows tedious and unproductive. However should I be able I too shall flee to Europe this fall.

I await the story. I am all eager to see it. Shoot it to me.

And Helene? What new poems are written or conceived. I would enjoy receiving some copies of recent effusions.

Have finished a book of essays entitled: Aunt Hagar's Children. It contains essays on Negro writers, Du Bois, Garvey, Washington, Douglass, and divers other subjects. And my new novel is progressing nicely if slowly,* and I am writing a talking movie. Please write to me both of you. I promise to write individual letters next time. Much love,

As always,
Wallie

**Infants of the Spring* (New York: Macaulay, 1932).

From: Wallace Thurman, Salt Lake City
To: Dorothy West

[Fall 1929?] Midnight Thursday

My Dear Dot:
Your letter came this afternoon. I answer during my first free moment. My grandmother is in the hospital having had a cataract removed to save the sight of her one good eye. My grandfather has migrated to Nevada after having lost his life time (?) job here in Salt Lake. Hence I am the official housekeeper. I feed the canaries, superintend their baths, feed the dog, and switch him temperately when he nips the heels of passersby, vacuum the rugs, prepare my own breakfast (dine in a restaurant), and today even cut the lawn as well as watered. It, the last item, was indeed a novel experience. It being my first attempt. The lawn's appearance eloquently incriminates me as an amateur.

My dear Dot I do not want you to become promiscuous nor to sacrifice your virginity purely because I ventured the opinion that it seemed to me your stories lacked passion and that your virginal state might be in some vague way responsible. I may, you know, be all wrong in both my opinions. Were I more certain I would be more rash with my prescriptions for immediate treatment. For if I was really assured that your limitation was the direct cause of being virginal I would see that you lost the status of a maiden even if I had to officiate at the ceremony.

But I grow facetious. What I do want you to do is not be like Helene, and for your intellect's sake get rid of the puritan notion that to have casual sexual intercourse is a sin. It's a biological necessity my dear. More tragedies result from girls clinging to their virginity than you would imagine. Physically, mentally it is bad after a certain age. Celibacy is certainly admirable under certain conditions and at certain times, but sex is after all but an expression of bodily hunger and must be appeased like the hunger of the stomach. Not immoderately of course, for gluttony is always harmful to one's physical and mental organs. But when one is hungry one should eat, and an 18 year fast may bring about chemical disturbances as the 18 day diet brings on acidosis. I don't say just saunter forth and give yourself to the first taker. I only say don't repress yourself, nor violently suppress your sex urge, just because you are Puritan enough to believe that hell fire awaits he who takes a bite of the apple, unless you are profoundly inoculated with the illusion of love. You might be too sensible to entertain that illusion, but you will certainly be subject to chemical affinity, and when the call comes do not wait to decide if this is *the* man. *The* man may never materialize or else be halted in his rush to you. And unplucked fruit soon loses its fragrance and rots. Be discreet but be adventurous is a good motto for the literary tribe.

About Helen? I wish you would tell me more. This is not idle curiosity. But I still do not know how she hurt her leg, and I do feel partially responsible for all that may have happened to her since I urged her into Harlem and wrote a rather silly letter after leaving her in Detroit.

About Simone. I cannot guess who she is positively, nor do I believe she is specifically any one person. I saw in her a composite of Cheryl and Georgette Harvey (God forgive me this patent disparity, but she seemed to have la belle Harvey's power and force of will and Cheryl's aesthetic pretensions). Am I by any chance luke warm? And did I not sense something of Edna Thomas* in Bersis? And Crown's Bess in

*Edna Thomas was a well-known actress. Johnson and West occasionally boarded with Thomas and her husband Lloyd.

Jessica. And is it possible on recapitulation to say that Simone is all Cheryl?

After Macaulay let's try Harper and all the rest. Somebody has to be congenial. I have written most eloquently to Mr. Furman of Macaulay's damning the easily published and untalented Fausets and Larsens[†] and pleading for recognition of potential talent from a newer and renovated generation.

Do write me again fulsomely and immediately. It's damn lonesome here and I do enjoy hearing from those whom I isolate as particularly beloved companions. The talkie lies dormant half finished. I'm not imbecilic enough yet for the movies, but the mood may come. And meanwhile my novel progresses apace.

Most affectionately, Wallie
Love to Helene.

[†]Harlem Renaissance novelists Jessie Fauset (1884–1961) and Nella Larsen (1893–1964).

New Orleans
From: Zora Neale Hurston, P.O. Box 5201, Station B,
To: Dorothy West, 43 W. 66th St., 2nd floor rear, NYC

[November 1929?]*

Dear Dorothy,
Wally should perk up. I know that it is annoying for his mother-in-law to keep on living and pestering him, but then there are gunmen down on the East Side who hire out for as low as $25.00. He should be a very happy man by Thanksgiving.

You are a love, Dot, no less, to put my parcel away so carefully. It is my fault for not wrapping better, and for not writing the letter first. It all turns out to be futile, for I must now take those duplicates I sent you and go to work from an entirely different angle than at first. Would you send me all the typed sheets, secretly, and by registered mail? I'll be eternally grateful if you will.

Of course you are near my heart and always will be. I trust you and Helene more than anyone else in the world. You are the fine gold in New York's show and shine. I have a lot in store for you.

I am O.K. in every way and hope to see you early in the year. But do not think of leaping out of 43.† I probably wont have time to stop long.

PLEASE DON'T LET ANYONE KNOW THAT YOU HAVE HEARD FROM ME OR SEE MY PAPERS BEFORE YOU MAIL THEM.

Lovingly yours,
Zora

*During this, her second visit to New Orleans, Hurston stayed all of November and part of December. By March of 1930 she was back in New York City (Hemenway, *Zora Neale Hurston*, 130).

† Hurston's former apartment. Johnson and West moved there the summer of 1927.

From: Helene Johnson, 470 Brookline Ave., Back Bay, Boston
To: Dorothy West, 43 W. 66th St., 2nd floor rear, NYC

Tuesday [3 December 1929]

Dot dear—
Have you got your Prologue yet? Please tell me if you haven't. It must have gone astray & I'll send you Daughter's.* Let me know.

Congratulations about Fannie Hurst. I feel sure that something splendid will come out of it.

Dorothy darling, you are a jewel. How did you ever happen to write to Irene B[ordoni]?† What did you say and everything. You must tell me all about it. Dot baby dear she wrote me the most beautiful letter, in French, 5 pages, and *glorious.* I'm sending it to you air mail special just as soon as I answer it. There's something nice about you in it Dimp. Oh Dot I love you for that. You're so perfect. I feel 600% happier & better and cheerfuller. Dot, how did you ever get the nerve to write to Irene all by yourself. Of course she's our friend, but gee, I'd have been scared to death Dot 'cause we love her so much & if she hadn't answered it would have been so sort of let-me-downish. Dot, anyone with your nerve has got to accomplish a simple little thing like selling a novel.

I wish I could do something as marvelous for you.

You must write to her and thank her, dear, because you write such beautiful letters & you know mine are so d—phlegmatic.

*Johnson's mother, Ella Benson Johnson (the oldest girl of her parents' children), was called Daughter.

†A French stage actress, Bordoni (1892–1953) made her Broadway debut in 1912 in "The Complex." Her obituary is in Daniel Blum's *Theatre World* (New York: Greenberg 1953).

Goodbye for the present darling. I'll send you a copy of the letter I send her.

Dot, you're a thoroughbred.

Tojours,

Helen

From: Helene Johnson, NYC
To: Dorothy West, 470 Brookline Ave., Back Bay, Boston

[Thursday, 23 October 1930]

Dear Dot,

I was awfully happy to hear from you Dot. I certainly do miss you. I shall look for places the first chance I get, but it gets dark so quickly now adays and Jene is so sweet I hate to let him know I want to move. He's the best man in this world. But of course I will tell him when the time comes, he's too good to treat low-down. I might come home for Thanksgiving. Zora may come, it will sort of make up for the beach. She is awfully crazy about you. She says her brother broke his engagement as he is really in love with you. He seems quite eligible, too. I haven't seen a soul. How is Minnie?* Tell her to keep her chin up. Hurry up and finish the old novel. Write to Zora sometimes, she thinks of you as her more or less wilful baby.

Love, Dimpsie, will write again. I hope we get a peach of a place.

Always your pal,
Helen

No that mysterious woman, Zora's boss,† does not know I'm working for Zora. Will let you know how it turns out.

*West and Johnson's Aunt Minnie Benson Rickson.
†Charlotte Mason, the wealthy widow of Dr. Rufus Osgood Mason.

From: Helene Johnson, 470 Brookline Ave., Back Bay, Boston
To: Dorothy West, 1890 Seventh Ave., Apt. 2A, NYC,
c/o Lloyd Thomas

Tuesday [24 February 1931]

Hello my little cousin,
This is just a note to tell you how well and happy everyone here at home is, and too, how much we all miss you. Why don't you come and see us sometime. I wish the carfare didn't cost so much. I have been thinking about my Dorothy & I think you ought to marry whoever you want no matter what he is like, if you love him. When you have your little baby, & Dot no matter when you marry, *your baby will be healthy,* you can do as you like about separation, but my little Darthy would make such a beautiful mother. The older we grow, the less illusions we have, & as far as abnormality goes, I don't think that's important at all. We may be ourselves, if we were in a different environment. Anyway, Dimp, once you had your baby, you'd have your whole future free & ready for your career. You'd be so complete. You'd be such a divine mother, Dimpsie.

. . . It is a beautiful day today. We're going to take some snaps of the white trees in the yard and send them to you. We are all so glad that you are happy and popular & in love. You have so many years for your writing, so few for love. After all, love after 30 or 35 does make one a bit ridiculous. Except you, you will always be as juicy as this year's spring & as lovely.

Your pal
Helen

From: Helene Johnson, 470 Brookline Ave., Back Bay, Boston
To: Dorothy West, 1890 Seventh Ave., Apt. 2A, NYC, c/o Lloyd Thomas

[2 March 1931]

Dear Dot,
This is just a note. I got your letter this morning. Dot darling, I don't know what to say about the dress. You see it's the only party dress I have, just like the beaded dress is the only party dress you have. It isn't as attractive on me as it is on you, but it is all the formal dress I have. And I think it is just as formal a dress as the beaded one, Dot. If you want to exchange it for the beaded one, ok. But do you think you should wear a white taffeta dress like that unless the men are going to be in tux, and isn't this going to be a tea? If it's a formal party as that, your own little beaded dress will be quite the thing. You look heavenly in that.

If I had another party dress I'd give you the white one in a jiffy, Dot. I believe you know that. But when I do get to N.Y. that party dress, that little yellow one Edna gave me, & my black velvet are all the clothes I have.

If you want something new, can't you pick up something at Klein's, or is it $? Has anyone seen your green chiffon with the little lace jacket? I love that, it's so flimsy & feminine. How about the velvet dress Edna gave you?

Am I awfully selfish, Dot? I don't mean to be, honestly. I love my cousin so much and I know how you feel about the tea & especially about the blonde boy.

I told Rae about the dress. There's no hard feelings, dear. I hope you will understand, too. I'm sure Ike will give you something so you can go to Klein's or if it is a real party party, wear your beaded dress and knock them all dead.

Brother is here tonite. Romane and John are sweet as can be. Awfully smart, they'd adore you, they tolerate me. Love to you, Dot. I know things are bound to come out your way. You can xchange dresses if you like, but you'd be getting the worse of the bargain I'm afraid. Don't be mad at your Pal,

H

From: Helene Johnson, 1890 Seventh Ave., Apt. 2A, NYC
To: Dorothy West, Meschrapborn Film Corp,
Moscow, U.S.S.R.

[Saturday, 15 October 1932]

My dearest little Darthy,
Let me know the minute you decide to go to Paris. Send a cable collect. Daughter says I can go. Please don't disappoint me. I've been in love again and you know what that means to me. I'm normal again now, tho, darling. I'd give half my life to be in Paris or somewhere away. Please don't forget me. I have enough clothes. I lost the job. If I don't have enough money extra, I'll borrow it. Please keep your word, Dot. I'm writing again. I think the stuff is the best I've done. I want you to see it. I know you've been writing. I'm so proud of you.

Don't come back home. Go to Paris. I'll leave so as to get there when you do. The rates are so cheap in the fall and winter. God, I could write.*

Take care of yourself, my little one.
Always your own
Helen

I do love you, little cousin. You're always so sane. Good luck to you.

*This trip to Europe never occurred, as West's father died in 1933 and she returned home to Boston.

From: Helene Johnson, 1890 Seventh Ave., Apt. 2A, NYC
To: Dorothy West, Meschrapborn Film Corp,
Moscow, U.S.S.R.

[Thursday, 8 December 1932]

Dearest of pals,
It is so good of you to remember me away over there in Russia. I am so happy when your letters reach me. I appreciate them specially when I know how difficult and almost impossible it must be to write to anyone at a time like this when your mind and your thoughts are with what is going on around you. Darling, you are just one great big peach. That is why you are some place today and me no place. Because you keep your word. You said you'd write and you did. I know I don't write as often as I should, but Dot I have you in mind all the time. But I know you know that. Did you move to the country? I rush to see all of the Russian movies, read all the Soviet articles in the newspapers and magazines, tho I wonder if the reading matter really does give an accurate picture of Russia. Dot baby, just imagine, you're a part of that great new economic laboratory, part of a splendid experiment, and I think before long that other countries will be following Russia's example; it's the only way out, oh Dot I can't help but envy you so much. Green Pastures' cast returned home yesterday. Your little friend, Al Thayer, comes over here all the time to play poker with Tommy, but I never see him, you can imagine how I run. Oh yes, I've been here at Tommy's for a week now.* One week today. Oh Dot, do you really think I can come to Germany. I am saving money, in the post office. There's not much wages to Molly's job, but quite good tips.

*Johnson was living with the married couple Lloyd and Edna Thomas. She calls Mrs. Edna Thomas, Tommy. Edna Thomas acted on Broadway and made a sensation as Lady Macbeth in the 1936 all-black production of *Macbeth*, at Harlem's Lafayette Theater.

I've developed quite a charming sunny disposition since you saw me, purely from a financial standpoint with a canny but grateful eye to tips. Nazimova and Edward Robinson might do Pearl Buck's "The Good Earth" for the Theatre Guild. I asked the post man for some quick way to send letters to Russia and he told me no. He said there was no air mail, but it was up in Harlem, so he may have just been dumb.

Oh Dot, if I could get to Germany. Please don't forget me. But I know you won't. Mr. West and I have good times together. We took Helyne Jones (629 Tinton Ave. Apt. 16 Bronx, NY—postcard) with us the last time. Ikey is having the time of his life down there by himself. I go to see him about 2 or 3 times a week after work and my day off I often spend with him. I put his sheets in the laundry and take awfully good care of your little papa. Oh Dot, but you must be happy.

Darling, on the contrary from gaining ten lbs. I've lost 10 lbs. Since I've been working, I only weigh 95. But I don't look half as anemic as that must sound. My skin looks great. I saw Rose McClendon[†] on 7th Ave the other day alone and wanted to speak to her so bad. She looked beautiful. But she wouldn't remember me. How is George Sample[‡] getting along? I should think Russia would be just the thing for him. After all he can take his bar exams practically any time, he's a rather nice person, and Russia ought to bring out the initiative and

[†]Perhaps the finest black actress of the 20s and 30s. She starred as Serena in the October 1927 debut of *Porgy* at New York City's Guild Theater.

[‡]Sample had traveled to Russia primarily to accompany his fiancée, Katherine Jenkins, a Convent Avenue housemate of Louise Thompson's. Thompson, who was briefly married to Wallace Thurman in 1928, was also on the Russian trip. See Arnold Rampersad's *The Life of Langston Hughes* (New York: Oxford University Press, 1986).

fineness in him. If he leaves the vodka casually alone. And how is Molly and Ted and Moon?[§] Dot, baby, you are the only faithful one, aren't you? Roberta wanted me to live with her, but you know of course how it had all been arranged with Tommy and I am very comfortable and content here. Particularly so since you and I lived in this room before. Inez' room is taken by someone named Jimmy Daniels, a young artist. I've never seen him. I come in so late. And Olivia has Joyce's bedroom. I heard unathoritatively, by that I mean overhearing on the telephone, ha, ha, that little Ross Cheyney had died following an operation. Isn't that a pity. I didn't know the baby but I heard you all speak of him so often. Zora is coming home so the 66th St. front stoop sages inform me, and will reside in the village. The village will really be more Zora's speed, she is such an individualist. She should have gone to Russia with you all with her knowledge of the African and the American Negro. Bobo wants me to marry him. He wanted to get the license last week, but I'd rather go to Germany and anyway he has no $ and he's about 40 and I know you'd never like him and he'd never get along with the Bensons tho he is a nice loyal kid.

Tallulah Bankhead[‖] in Thunder Below with Chas. Bickford was not so hot. The little lady is a bit too sullen and morbid looking for me, without Garbo's spirituality and Dietrich's strange photographic charm. I'll bet in private life tho she's gorgeous.

[§]Journalists Ted Poston and Henry Lee Moon worked for the *Amsterdam News*. Molly Lewis was a graduate of Columbia University's Teachers' College.

[‖]Bankhead was a popular performer during the Harlem Renaissance. She was born in Huntsville, Alabama, in January of 1902.

I am writing again. Honestly. I'll have lots of things to show you when I see you. Oh Dot, will I really see you in Germany? Jean is fine. Tell Molly please to write to Jean.# Jean was so fond of her and still is. She is 580 St Nicholas Ave. Apt 2–A. I sure miss my little cousin. Would you like to have me send you something? Do you ever get homesick? Foolish questions #101, I spose. Have you worn the little white dress I gave you? Tell Molly to give you that old brown sport coat I gave her. You'd look awfully cute in it and I'm mad on Molly because she sent all those Nordics at the theatre a card and not me, and was I embarrassed, you know how white people are, they think our kind like them a little bit better than their own, anyway. Here I come with my American color point of view. Why bring that up, eh, Dot? I guess you thought you'd about finished with that rot when you touched Russia. How does it really feel to be a woman and not a curiosity? How is charming Langston?** I suppose he is piling up material by the store. And you, Dot. Don't neglect your work, you're the only woman creative artist in the group, aren't you? I can hardly wait to see you. I've read lots and I've got lots of excerpts to copy and send you. You won't read them but I'll love sending them.

Thank you again for your very great kindness in remembering me so loyally. You are so true, Dot. Good luck

#Eugenia (Jean) Rickson was West and Johnson's first cousin.

**Langston Hughes (1902–1967) was the most prolific and among the most gifted of the Harlem Renaissance writers.

come to you and stay with you and love to you, little Darthy, and to all of you. Love again, and lots of it,

Always, your own
Helene

From: Helene Johnson, 1890 Seventh Ave., Apt. 2A, NYC
To: Dorothy West, Meschrapborn Film Corp,
Moscow, U.S.S.R.

April 24, 1933
Monday

Dearest Dimpsie,

Darling little cousin, Tommy is sending you this $5 for your birthday and she sends with it all her good wishes and all her love. She is very good to me, darling Dimp, and she is your really and truly fine friend.

I cabled you to come home against my own wishes, dear, but because the family wants you back so. You've been away so long, darling, and they are worried about you and I'm afraid to have you stay over there so far from home or my responsibility. I love you and want you to stay and work hard and make good, things are so terrible over here, but you know how families are.

Of course you stay with me Dot when you return. Ray* wants you to live at Inez' but I think you and I would have lots of fun together here and Tommy and Lloyd and Olivia and Al Thayer and all your own particular and dearest friends want you back here. They all miss you so. Geo. Bernard Shaw's been over here since you've been gone. We can go to Oak Bluffs too after the crowd goes or after they're there. Darling, you'll be the catch of the season.

It will be wonderful, seeing you again, Dot dear. Take good care of yourself and do as you think best about returning. I wish they'd just give you a return ticket. The family wants you back awfully bad. We all miss you and love you.

Love to you, always and always, your own Big Cousin,

Helene

*West's mother, Rachel.

From: Zora Neale Hurston, 1925 7th Ave, Apt 2J, NYC

To: Dorothy West, 43 W. 66th St, NYC

Postcard

[Monday] 22 March 1937

Dear Dot,

I would love to see you. Phone not connected yet. I will be in. Come a running, honey.*

Zora

*Hurston had just returned from the West Indies where three months earlier, in December 1936, she had finished writing her classic novel *Their Eyes Were Watching God*.

From: Abigail Hubbell, 81 No. Portland Ave., Brooklyn
To: Rachel West, Oak Bluffs, Massachusetts

[Wed, 4 February 1948]

Dear Ray,
Thank you so much for the sweater. It fits perfectly. I wish I could send you something just as nice. Well I am going out at last. The very first day I went ice skating and almost broke my nose against an iron fence. When I grow up I am going to drive a bob sled. I am so heavy. I am the only girl who goes down the icy run in our park. I weigh 81 pounds now. But I am not fat. I am almost tall as Daughter. I have my own library card. My canary sings so sweet. He got loose twice. He got behind the stove and now his tail is all black and it wont come off. We threw a hat over him to catch him. But he still sings. I still have the dolls you made for me. The two wooden ones stand up on the window sill and the cloth ones sit up.

Love
Abigail

Afterword

A Daughter Reminisces

When Helen died, there were stacks and stacks of her handwritten works all over the room, under the bed, in closets, in drawers, behind bureaus. I gathered them and put them into boxes. It seemed as if her works were going to be buried with her. Nobody had any interest in the new epistles from this ancient, reclusive, "minor" literary talent.

Then Cheryl called, then Mitch, then Clark, and suddenly Helen was getting what she had always wanted, "attention to the work and not the person" despite her refusal to cooperate.

Much has been written about our being "Boston Brahmins" and people of "privilege." Well, there can be no question that for a while we were a family of substance, but by the time I came along, we were shabby gentility at best. Helen never aspired to be rich, that was Dorothy's thing. (It should be mentioned that three of the cousins, Helen, Dorothy, and Jean, worked together in raising me; but early on Jean moved to Ohio and most of the task was left to Helen and Dorothy. I was born when they were late in life and have had pressure on me to fulfill each of their dreams ever since the forceps hit my noggin.) Helen always said, you can lose your money but not your brains, which is probably why I keep marrying smart men instead of rich ones. In any case, a word should be said about the family economics since the only written evidence we have is Dorothy's version in *The Living Is Easy,* which caused such a catastrophic uproar in the family that most members stopped speaking to Dorothy. To this day many family members still don't speak to one another as a direct result of that book.

It is true that Isaac West, Dorothy's father, was a businessman. In fact, he was the only man in the family at that time. He had a fruit and vegetable store and proclaimed himself the Banana King of Boston. But what is left out is that all of the sisters (all nine of them) pitched in together in a communal way in order to maintain a lifestyle which had the facade of the real Boston Brahmins.

The girls had a Finnish governess and did not go to school with other children until they were "molded." They knew their Goethe, Schiller, and Shakespeare. At night, they would write pieces and read them aloud at the end of the evening as entertainment. When I first read *Little Women,* it was the faces of the "girls" that I envisioned. They went to the theater, joined writing clubs, and did all of the cultural things that young ladies of privilege did, except they did it with the resources pooled together by all three mothers and several aunts. Aunt Carrie, best known as Dolly, didn't even have children. They were a kibbutz, a commune, and the big house in Boston and the beach house at Martha's Vineyard were part of the large family collective.

All of the mothers were in service except Rachel. Which meant that Rachel took care of the girls while the others went to work as maids. In those days, maids would work for weeks at a time before they would have a day off to visit their families. One of my mother's earliest memories was seeing her mother walk off in the morning to go to work. Helen would watch her until she disappeared into the horizon. Then she would turn from the window to find that she was left with Rachel. When you were left with Rachel, you were alone with no one on your side. Rachel was formidable. She was extremely intelligent—could cite any line from Shakespeare—and extremely mean. Why she was mean is another story. The fact that she was mean and gave those girls a life of high intellect and misery is key. Each girl grew up with life-long negative reactions to Rachel and motherhood. Only Helen was brave enough to have a child. Poor Rachel, she did all the right things, but somehow, her bitterness clouded all of her actions. When I say that Rachel was formidable, I am not kidding around.

Helen was one of the few writers of the Harlem Renaissance to have a child. She worked hard at being a good mother, and succeeded at being one of the best. She was a marvel. She broke all of the conventional rules and had a great time doing it.

It is difficult to remember the first rule my mother broke. She broke so many of them that it is almost easier to dwell on the moments in my youth when she did not break a rule. But those instances, and I'm sure there must have been some, are few and very far between.

Let us say that my mother, the poet, was extremely eccentric. Even though she had stopped writing poetry on a professional level before I was born, she continued to live life with the soul of a poet until she died. And, moreover, she wrote a little something every day of her life, even if it was an ad for a car ("Cadillac is Badillac") or a review for a film.

I remember that as an infant I had a perambulator that was very expensive. I mean extraordinarily expensive. Expensive enough so that well-heeled upper-class people would think twice about it. It was made in England and had huge wheels and a trap door. How do I remember this you may ask? Because Helen wheeled me in it until I was five years old. When I was six, in first grade mind you, I used to push my dollies in it and occasionally, on long walks, my mother would move the dollies over and throw me in it as well.

I clearly remember coming home late one evening after a walk across the Brooklyn Bridge, and being pushed by my mom to our apartment in the Fort Green housing projects. Now, our neighbors didn't really care about how expensive the white pram was; they only thought it was weird that I was still being pushed in it. And that night, Butch Anselmo shouted out, "Look! Abby's still being pushed like a baby."

When I was outside with the other kids, Helen used to bring down chocolate milk with a poorly disguised egg in it. This was before blenders but not before eggbeaters, which we had. Still she would beat the egg with a fork, add the milk and Hershey's chocolate syrup, and then bring it to me in an old Hellmann's mayonnaise jar that still had some black crud around the waxy cardboard inner thing. Meanwhile all the other kids were having Cokes and Mountain Dews. The trouble here, aside from the obvious, was that she mixed it so poorly that you could see the streaks of the yolk, and the albumin was always floating around. I never noticed anything wrong with it until good old Butch Anselmo pointed it out to me with an "EWWW! Look at that, Abby is drinking a raw egg."

Butch and I were later discovered playing doctor in the back of the house by Ilma Watkins, my best friend's mother. I had a feeling I was doing something wrong by the way Butch was being nice to me, but I knew I was doing something wrong by Ilma's reaction to the scene. That night after dinner, Helen (yes, I called my mother Helen) made cutout paper dolls, something we often did together, only this night, she filled in the previously blank body parts. I was either six or seven at the time and didn't know much, but I did know that this was a departure and that the lecture she was giving me was important. But I had no idea what she was talking about. Anyway, after that I used to make all my cutout dolls with full genitalia. In school, P.S. 67, the teacher, Mrs. Aranold, was very cool about it and called my mother in. I don't know what happened, but the next year I went to the very progressive private school, The Little Red Schoolhouse, on a very large scholarship. When Mrs. Aranold was later fired for being a communist, Helen initiated a picket line around the school to have her reinstated. A big problem here was that she was the only one on the line.

Helen used to accuse me of "ghetto thinking," and because we were black and we lived in a housing project in Brooklyn, I always assumed that it meant thinking from the bottom up instead of from the top down. It was not until I was about ten years old that I discovered what she meant. She meant that my thinking was controlled by boundaries, that I was encircled by limitations in the same manner that a geographical ghetto is within boundaries. What she wanted me to realize is that with imagination there are no limitations to thought. Once I was able to understand this, I could see how limitless life was and how all things were possible. And since I have always been a big showoff, I went and accused Sondra Johnson of having ghetto thinking, with the assumption that I could expand her horizons. Instead she punched me out.

The traditional Christmas experience in our household was to get the tree at the very last minute on Christmas Eve. It was the belief that we would provide a warm and loving home for the trees that "went begging." Helen had convinced me that if we didn't take these trees home, they would never know the joys of being trimmed and bringing happiness to families. The big plump full trees always found a loving home, but the skinny bedraggled ones were left to sprawl on the cold cement sidewalk, naked and unloved on Christmas Day. So, it was an act of humanitarianism for us to take them in, sometimes two or three tied together to look like one normal-sized one. I believed in this tradition with all of my heart. Never doubted it for one moment. It came as a complete shock to me when my son married and his wife forbid him to carry on the tradition. Only then did he tell me that the reason for this "tradition" was that the trees were free. It took me a long time to digest this, but I have finally come to accept it. My mother and I were never poor; we were always "broke." Now that I think about it, of course, my son was right. We would be carrying these trees on the subway after midnight with one pair of mittens between us. But the myth of doing good had become so strong that it never occurred to me that it was an act of charity for me and not the tree.

Helen took me to the ballet starting when I was two-and-a-half years old. According to her, I never squirmed, never fidgeted, and always watched intently and quietly. We started going to the opera when I was around ten. Helen explained that the reason we always took standing room was that it gave us the opportunity to move around to the music. Something the confines of an orchestra seat could not do. At the end of the first act, someone would invariably give us their tickets in the expensive orchestra seats, and although Helen would take them, she explained to me that we were doing them a favor giving up our standing-room spaces. We had had our time moving around and it would be rude to refuse them.

Once an usher actually came up to us and asked to see our tickets. Helen flashed them on her with such disdain that one would have thought she was a patron.

Helen was always very casual about her famous past. A kind of Boston shy arrogance. I say arrogance because although she never told me who they were in history, by the time I was eight, she somehow expected me to know who Zora and Wally (Wallace Thurman) were. So I faked it. She would tell stories about Alain (Locke) and Langston (Hughes) without ever giving their last names. Somehow I grew up not having any idea at all that these people were legends. To me they were characters in family stories.

I used to hear Helen and Dorothy talking about Zora, but they never told me who she was. I knew that she was an anthropologist, but I thought that she was an anthropologist and a writer who made fun of black people. Gimme a break, I was only around eight when I became aware of her. Zora was the hotshot among the women. She had her own apartment at 111 Lenox Avenue and an income from a mysterious source, which allowed her to spend most of her time writing. The fact is that Zora subcontracted out the jobs from the mysterious source to Helen so that she could do her own work. Zora also subleased her apartment to the "girls." They were scared to tell their parents that they were living "on their own," so they kept their room at the Harlem YWCA and continued to get their mail there. Their folks never found out that they were living unchaperoned in Harlem.

Zora was the real deal; like Dorothy, she talked more than she wrote and she was a fantastic mimic. Although she was working class and loud, she was ten times smarter and more prolific than anyone else and the men were very jealous of her. There was much speculation as to whether or not Zora had to be as "earthy" as she was. After all, her mom taught school and her dad was a minister. Dorothy was convinced that Zora "acted a fool" in order to get commissions. Helen thought that Zora was naturally like that since being middle class in Eatonville, Florida, was not quite the same as being middle class in Boston. Which is why I grew up thinking that Zora was another educated person telling stories about undereducated people. Somebody told me that when Zora died she was working as a maid back in Florida. Had it not been for Alice Walker, her work would have died with her as well.

I want to express my gratitude to Verner Mitchell for unearthing my mother's work. Helen's work, like Zora's, is too vibrant, too funny, too political, and too right-on to be buried in the back of my closet.

Abigail McGrath
New York City, 2000

Selected Bibliography

The following list is a guide, rather than a complete bibliography, to works that discuss Helene Johnson's life and art.

Bennett, Gwendolyn. "The Ebony Flute." *Opportunity* (September 1926): 292–93; (October 1926): 322–23; (December 1926): 391; (January 1927): 29; (July 1927): 212–13.

Bryan, T. J. "Helene Johnson." In *Notable Black American Women*, ed. Jessie Carney Smith, 587–591. Detroit: Gale, 1992.

———. "The Published Poems of Helene Johnson." *The Langston Hughes Review* 6.2 (Fall 1987): 11–21.

Dalsgård, Katrine. "Alive and Well and Living on the Island of Martha's Vineyard: An Interview with Dorothy West, October 29, 1988." *The Langston Hughes Review* 12.2 (Fall 1993): 28–44.

Ferguson, Sally Ann H. "Dorothy West and Helene Johnson in *Infants of the Spring*." *The Langston Hughes Review* 12.2 (Fall 1993): 22–24.

"Helene Johnson." In *Call and Response: The Riverside Anthology of the African American Literary Tradition*, ed. Patricia Liggins Hill, et al., 916–23. New York: Houghton Mifflin, 1998.

"Helene Johnson." In *The Norton Anthology of African American Literature*. Ed. Henry Louis Gates, Nellie Y. McKay, et al. New York: W. W. Norton, 1997. 1315–18.

"Helene V. Johnson." In *Anthology of Magazine Verse for 1926*, ed. William Stanley Braithwaite, 22. Boston: B. J. Brimmer, 1926.

Honey, Maureen. *Shadowed Dreams: Women's Poetry of the Harlem Renaissance.* New Brunswick: Rutgers University Press, 1989.

Hull, Gloria T. "Black Women Poets from Wheatley to Walker." In *Sturdy Black Bridges: Visions of Black Women in Literature*, ed. Roseann P. Bell, Bettye J. Parker, and Beverly Guy-Sheftall, 69–86. Garden City, N.Y.: Anchor, 1979.

Johnson, James Weldon. *The Book of American Negro Poetry.* 1931. New York: Harcourt, 1983.

McDowell, Deborah E. "Conversations with Dorothy West." In *The Harlem Renaissance Re-examined*, ed. Victor A. Kramer, 265–82. New York: AMS Press, 1987.

Miller, Nina. *Making Love Modern: The Intimate Public Worlds of New York's Literary Women.* New York: Oxford University Press, 1998.

Patterson, Raymond R. "Helene Johnson." In *Dictionary of Literary Biography.* Vol. 51. Ed. Thadious Davis and Trudier Harris, 164–67. Detroit: Gale, 1987.

——. "Helene Johnson." In *The Oxford Companion to Women's Writing in the United States*, eds. Cathy Davidson and Linda Wagner-Martin, 447–48. New York: Oxford University Press, 1995.

Perry, Margaret. *Silence to the Drums: A Survey of the Literature of the Harlem Renaissance.* Westport, Conn.: Greenwood, 1976.

Primeau, Ronald. "Frank Horne and the Second Echelon Poets of the Harlem Renaissance." In *The Harlem Renaissance Remembered*, ed. Arna Bontemps, 247–67. New York: Dodd, 1972.

Redmond, Eugene B. *Drumvoices: The Mission of Afro-American Poetry, A Critical History.* Garden City, N.Y.: Anchor, 1976.

Roses, Lorraine Elena and Ruth Elizabeth Randolph. *Harlem Renaissance and Beyond: Literary Biographies of 100 Black Women Writers, 1900–1945.* Boston: G. K. Hall, 1990.

Stetson, Erlene. *Black Sister: Poetry by Black American Women, 1746–1980.* Bloomington: Indiana University Press, 1985.

Wall, Cheryl A. *Women of the Harlem Renaissance.* Bloomington: Indiana University Press, 1995.

West, Dorothy. *The Richer, The Poorer.* New York: Anchor, 1995.

——. "Voices." *Challenge* 1.3 (May 1935): 46.

Index of Titles

The Harlem Renaissance Poems

Selected Poems—After the Harlem Renaissance

About the Authors

VERNER D. MITCHELL is a native of Thomasville, Georgia, the birthplace of West Point's first African American graduate, Lt. Henry O. Flipper. Like Flipper, but one hundred years later, Mitchell graduated from a service academy, the U.S. Air Force Academy, in 1979. A career officer and veteran of the Gulf War, he is, at present, an assistant professor of English at the University of Memphis. Mitchell writes on American literature and culture.

CHERYL A. WALL is professor and chair of the Department of English at Rutgers University. A pioneering critic of black women's literature, she edited the two-volume Library of America edition of Zora Neale Hurston's writings. Her *Women of the Harlem Renaissance* charts the artistic journeys of such women as Jessie Redmon Fauset, Gwendolyn Bennett, Bessie Smith, Nella Larsen, and Helene Johnson.

ABIGAIL MCGRATH is a casting director for independent feature films. She is also a screenwriter and script doctor and an instructor at New York University. Her stage plays have been produced in New York City, Martha's Vineyard, and California.